KNOWING THE UNKNOWABLE GOD

Knowing the Unknowable God:
Ibn-Sina, Maimonides, Aquinas

David B. Burrell, C.S.C.

University of Notre Dame Press
Notre Dame, Indiana 46556

Library of Congress Cataloging in Publication Data

Burrell, David B.
    Knowing the unknowable God.

    Includes index.
    1. God—History of doctrines.   2. Avicenna,
980–1037—contributions in the doctrine of God.
3. Maimonides, Moses, 1135–1204—Contributions
in the doctrine of God.   4. Thomas Aquinas, Saint,
1225?–1274—Contributions in the doctrine of God.
I. Title.
BL205.B87   1986   291.2'11'09   85–40600
ISBN 0-268-01225-3

Manufactured in the United States of America

To the Memory of
BERNARD J. F. LONERGAN, S.J.
1904–1984
Mentor and Liberator

Contents

Preface

THIS STUDY OF Ibn-Sina, Maimonides, and Aquinas intends to show how Muslim, Jew and Christian conspired to fashion a doctrine of God by transforming classical philosophy to display divine transcendence. The study is historical to the extent necessary to recover a medieval climate far more open to interfaith and intercultural exchange than our stereotypes have presumed it to be. Its aim is more contemporary and philosophical: to show us how to appropriate our own past in such a way as to profit by all that currently situates western Christians in conversation with other religious and cultural heritages. I owe this manner of appropriating past figures in our tradition to my mentor, Bernard Lonergan; while the explicit attention to other traditions was given expression by Karl Rahner in a lecture at Boston College in 1979.[1] Both men have served us well in showing how fruitful and liberating it can be to attempt to understand those who have gone before us in an effort to discover our own ways into the future. Such is the goal of this study, undertaken in the conviction that philosophical theology must henceforth entail a comparative inquiry among major religious traditions.

My recent mentors in matters Jewish and Muslim have been many, profiting as I have from two years in Jerusalem (1980-82) and two subsequent summers at the Institut Dominicain des Etudes Orientales in Cairo. I have always been instructed by the writings of Alexander Altmann and gained fresh perspective from repeated conversations with

Marcel Dubois, O.P. The hospitality of the Dominicans in
Cairo is legendary, and my indebtedness to Georges
Anawati, O.P., will be clear, though the witness of others
there, notably Jacques Jomier, O.P., deserves special men-
tion as well. My teachers of Arabic—Ibrahim Yannon
(Jerusalem) and Nazih Daher (Notre Dame)—must be cred-
ited for their patience with an older student.

I have transliterated key Arabic terms without additional
vowel or consonant markings in a spirit of economy:
Arabists will recognize them and others would find the
markings superfluous. Similarly, references to the writings
of Thomas Aquinas are abbreviated and given without distinguishing question from article, though the order will be
perspicuous to anyone wishing to consult the reference:
thus *ST* 1.11.1.1 = *Summa theologiae,* Part I, question 11,
article 1, response to objection 1. In general I have adopted
the translations given in the Blackfriars Latin-English edition of the *Summa* (London: Eyre and Spotiswoode,
1964). Translations from Ibn-Sina's *al-Shifa* give page and
line references (e.g. 380:11-12) to the edition by Georges
Anawati, O.P., (Cairo: Government Printing Office, 1936).

My final gratitude to the faculty steno pool at Notre
Dame, who saw the text through several emendations, and
especially to James Langford, Director of the University
of Notre Dame Press, whose vision welcomed publishing
this new venture of mine, and whose fine editorial hand
brought that risk to its completion.

Introduction

IT REMAINS A NICE question whether one can treat of God prescinding from any religious tradition, for should one try to do so, the implicit moorings of the discussion may betray the tradition one attempted to leave behind. I prefer to be more straightforward, acknowledging that humankind's primary relations with divinity occur in religious settings, and that the major religious communities have also developed sophisticated patterns of reflection on that interaction. It would be foolish, in the name of a pretended objectivity, to try to proceed in philosophical theology without the intellectual assistance of those traditions of faith.

That is especially true in an essay of conceptual clarification like this one, where one seeks to know what it is one is speaking of in speaking of God, how to relate this divinity to whatever else we may know, and how especially to handle the religious traditions' avowal that God lies beyond our ken. That recognition identifies the God we shall be inquiring into as the God of Abraham: of Isaac and Jacob as well as of Jesus, and of Muhammad. For it is Jews, Christians, and Muslims who share the burden, if you will, of the one God, creator of heaven and earth, and Lord of all. Moreover, it was the intellectual intermingling of these three traditions which made possible the medieval synthesis which has served as the baseline for western

1

theology ever since. Writing from within the middle tradition, I shall nevertheless show how its self-understanding
was formed in interaction with Judaism and Islam, and can
be enriched by recalling the dynamics of that formation.

The central figure in this drama is Thomas Aquinas, for
his utilization of Maimonides (Moses ben Maimon) and of
Avicenna (Ibn-Sina) mark two significant stages in clarifying the grammar of divinity and the disciplined use of
human language in speaking of God. By "the grammar of
divinity" I mean the proper formulation of divinity as
distinct from whatever else that is. For, it must be remem-
bered, each of these traditions asserts God to be "the
beginning and end of all things, and of rational creatures
especially." And from that description follows the startling
"distinction" of God from "all things," with the yet more
startling corollary that all those things add nothing to
God's perfection.

If the status of intentional creator places God outside
"all things" as their "beginning and end," then divinity
must be said to be outside that universe which forms the
context for all that we know and do: *ha-olam.* And so God
must be deemed unknowable, since we will not be able to
characterize the divine essence as we do things in the world
such as events, objects, species, numbers, or *jinn.* So the
quintessential theological task becomes one of formulating
that "distinction" so as to assure the required transcendence, while allowing us to have some notion of what it is
we are referring to in addressing "the Holy One," "our
Father," or "Allah Akbar." The reflective spirits in these
traditions must show how such address is misdirected if we
presume the one named to be among the store of things in
the world, yet in doing so they are but formulating the
intention of the faith-communities themselves. So their
goal is properly theological, yet the task remains one of
conceptual clarification, so the enterprise is properly called
"philosophical theology."[1]

I have called this quest for the proper characterization

of divinity "knowing the unknowable God," to remind us that we must always work with "the distinction" in mind. Nor can it simply be a matter of getting that distinction straight, once and for all, so that we would ever after be able to employ *that* formulation as a kind of algorithm to modify all subsequent statements. That cannot be hoped for because this distinction is unlike any other which we make to understand things in the world, for each of these, however formal, presumes the world as its background.[2] So we will have to proceed by negation rather than division; indeed each of the expressions which Aquinas uses to characterize those formal features which he will conjoin to give a unique characterization of divinity, is itself a negative term. Without pretending to offer a commentary on his way of construing these issues, I shall nonetheless be guided by what I have perceived to be Aquinas' structuring of the matter.[3] Moreover, the rationale for that structuring will consistently be presented in the light of the major Jewish and Muslim thinkers of the epoch—Maimonides, Ibn-Sina, and al-Ghazali—as a way of testing the adequacy of this approach to securing "the distinction."

The aim, then, is to secure the distinction of God from the world, and to do so in such a way as to display how such a One, who must be unknowable, may also be known. The exercise is clearly a philosophical one, however theological be its goal. It must also be historical, if we hope to gain from the sophistication developed in three religious traditions associated with "monotheism."[4] Yet the medieval crucible of exchange will be presented as an object lesson for our understanding of the matter at hand, rather than an inquiry of its own. To borrow a useful pair of terms, the study will incorporate *diachronic* and *synchronic* elements, in a necessary effort of conceptual clarification for us historical creatures.

Questions of interpretation will invariably dog us, yet the route to understanding lies in offering plausible interpretations, submitting them to criticism, and thereby

contributing to our critical self-awareness in such matters.⁵
To do that is to acknowledge oneself part of a continuing
community of discourse which reaches back well beyond
the medieval figures in question to their sources, and out
to fellow inquirers—especially Jews, Christians, and
Muslims, but others as well, and "non-believers" alike. For
the distinction in question lies at the margins of human
understanding and so at the intersection of reason with
faith—a locus one may well be aware of without being able
to inhabit.⁶

1. Picturing the Connection

BEFORE SCRUTINIZING THE distinction of God from the world it would seem best to consider their connection. Indeed, some would want us first to concern ourselves with establishing such a connection. And it is true that the vast majority of endeavors in philosophy of religion over the past few centuries in the west have been devoted to ways of confirming creation. That is, for the most part, what arguments purporting to exhibit God's existence intend. Even those which pretend to proceed not from effect to cause but from interior analysis of the notion of divinity, will not only begin with beings as we find them, but must conclude to a being whose very being gives existence to all that is. As Kant showed how the more familiar "cosmological" arguments implicitly embodied the notion of God demanded by their "ontological" counterparts, so we might remind ourselves how these more recondite analyses presuppose as their conceptual background the notion of creator—or at least a One from which emanates all that is.[1]

Yet for all these efforts, the connection turns out to be less something we can establish than it is something which imposes itself on us. And that fact will become more comprehensible the better we grasp the distinction. Kant's capstone concern whether—even were one successful—the first principle obtained would be a divinity we could worship, suggests one import of the distinction.[2] A more metaphysical way of putting it would be to ask how one *establishes* what one deems to be the floor upon which one operates, and this logical query animates proposals reflecting a spectrum of philosophical tempers: from God as a "basic belief" to what is presupposed to a specific way of life.[3]

In any case, the "proofs" must invariably involve a reflexive moment, when one presumes to assess the way we consider whatever we consider, and this move cannot help but render them suspect as *proofs*.[4] (Again understanding the distinction will clarify this moment.) As a result, many have taken refuge in a decision—or less coherently, a "fundamental option"—yet "decisions" of such moment represent more a cumulative awareness than a discrete action, so Newman's notion of "converging lines of probable reasoning" comes more and more to the fore.[5] And in such cases, it turns out that we seldom, if ever, reason *to* God's existence, but rather retrospectively retrace our tracks to satisfy ourselves of the cogency of the individual steps which cumulatively brought us to where we are.

This essay, at any rate, will presume such a perspective on foundational matters and it will display that presumption by showing how a gathering awareness of the import of "the distinction" renders that perspective increasingly plausible. In fact, we shall find ourselves wondering how we (or so many others) had so long been captured by another. There remains, however, what I shall dare to call a yet more fundamental issue, though it is less strictly a conceptual one. I shall call it "picturing the connection."

1.1   Background and Imagination

A theme common to attempts to convey the secular ethos of our time, especially by contrast to that of "premodern" times, highlights the absence of an enveloping tapestry in which we can locate ourselves.[6] It is precisely the shift from a cosmology accessible to imagination—and rendered fruitfully present, say, by Dante—to one which leaves the imagination with a vast emptiness. We may fill the void, of course, with science fiction, or let that endeavor be fleshed out for us with archetypal themes—as in Tolkien—yet the fact remains that we are doing it. Some would trace this imaginative impasse to Galileo, and hence to the modes of conceptualization inherent to modern science and only accentuated by Einstein's relativizing it all; others will find it focused in Freud, for whom a rootless individual must come to terms with a senseless cosmos.

In any case, the "crisis in meaning" which secularity represents, embodies a crisis of imagination which only dawns upon most of us when the events of our time cumulate to challenge our capacity to imagine *evil*. Auschwitz epitomizes what has become our preoccupation: how can we retain what we deem most precious—human life with human relationships—when that very gift can be systematically *eliminated* by totalitarian regimes, or made administratively to *disappear* by their authoritarian counterparts? And are not such callous "procedures" but the political consequence of our metaphysical malaise: how sustain our conviction that this is what is most precious—human life with its attendant relationships—when its origins and our imaginative hold on its sense vanish into a swirling void?[7]

Philosophers, and the philosopher in us all, will resist such vertiginous language, but does not our collective imagination— or our collective incapacity to imagine— hold us all in thrall? Are we not carried to that point where we must acknowledge the centrality of imagination in such ultimate (or religious) matters?[8] Yet what can all this possibly have to do with that distinction of God from the world, which must certainly outreach our imaginations? Indeed, as we shall see, attempts to imagine the distinction invariably betray it. Furthermore, the effort to articulate this distinction, above all, has always been recognized to be a properly metaphysical task, especially by those skeptical of such endeavors, and Aquinas could not be more forceful in reminding us that entering upon metaphysics means entertaining discriminations quite beyond our capacity to imagine.[9]

I shall answer that question indirectly, by sketching the background picture shared by Jewish, Christian, and Muslim religious thinkers up to the thirteenth century, in an effort to invoke its power as a picture. What first appears *to us* as a collective piece of science fiction can suddenly refocus as an entirely plausible picture. Yet *picture* it remains; those who received it as an account, we shall see, could find refuge in it from the rigors of "the distinction." It is not replaceable, certainly, but we will better appreciate how its absence can actually help us in our effort to formulate the distinction the more we realize the role that picture played. Aquinas' part in the drama becomes the more crucial as we realize how his grasp of the distinction unravelled the pattern of the grand tapestry, even though Dante would still picture the pilgrim's journey culminating in that "love which moved the sun and moon and all the stars."[10]

1.2 An Imaginative Scheme

While logicians prefer to concentrate on "argument" as the primary means of advancing our understanding, structuralists have long been reminding us of the role which schemes or patterns play—often precisely in licensing or facilitating particular paths for inference to take.[11] These are often less in evidence than are overt chains of reasoning; sometimes they are nothing more than the fashions of an age, which deem certain questions worth treating and others settled or irrelevant. More significantly, such patterns can represent the varying weight we give to different forms of argument, and so be illustrated by methodological reflections like Aristotle's opening observations in the

Ethics about the various meanings which 'precise' or 'rigorous' should assume as we undertake different sorts of inquiry. In this sense, we might consider the schemes I will be displaying as conveying what we *value* in inquiring.

What we may justly call "the classical scheme" grew out of that neo-platonic harmony of Aristotle with Plato legitimized by passing on Books I-II of the *Enneads* of Plotinus as the "Theology of Aristotle." The result was an articulated emanation from the One of diverse levels of spiritual substances (more or less identified in the heavenly bodies) culminating in the Agent Intellect, whose role was to enlighten human beings regarding their place in the cosmos by illuminating them regarding all that lay above and below them. The levels of intelligences, moreover, offered a paradigm for those same human beings in their noblest practical endeavor: politics. So the scheme not only linked nature with spirit, the structure of the cosmos with a theory of knowledge, but provided a pattern for action as well by properly subordinating practical to speculative knowing.

Presented with such an elaboration, we are usually so puzzled as to ask: did they really *believe* this is how things are? What could they possibly have proffered as evidence? And curiously enough, they bring forth little by way of evidence; the Arabs in particular seem more concerned with elaborating the scheme than with establishing it, and it passed neatly from Alfarabi to Ibn-Sina with some minor alterations.[12] They "took it on faith," it seems, as embodying the teaching of "philosophy," and as representing the connection between the first cause—primal being (or God)— and all that we see or know. Moreover, the ten cosmic spheres represented that connection mediately, so facilitating the move from One to many, all the while preserving the axiom: from One only one can come.[13]

Now the logical sleight of hand involved in reducing the scandal of many in the face of One by the simple ruse of adding intermediaries should alert us that something other than argument is going on here. In fact, as we shall see, it is less a matter of "how the world is" than it is how we should relate to what is. The cosmological components seem not to be important in themselves (as *assertions* of how things are) so much as in establishing a parallel between nature and knowing, so that the world, and especially our place in it, will be intelligible enough to lead *us* onto the proper return path to the One—by way of contributing to a virtuous city by actively imitating the pattern, or of consciously retracing the steps of emanation from the One so that we contemplate our origin as our goal. The scheme serves as an aid to self-consciousness by properly locating us in the overall scheme of things, and indicates how we should fulfill that self (our nature) by active or contemplative paths —a judicious blend of Plato's *Republic* with Aristotle's *Politics*.[14]

We are in the presence, then, of an intellectual scheme which purportedly speaks of the natures of things, designed rather to offer a background image of the connection between God and the world, and hence a pattern for our activity within that world and under that God. Such is the interpretation suggested by Joel Kraemer's essay tracing the structural similarities among John of Damascene, Alfarabi, and Moses Maimonides in their elaboration of and the use to which they put a common scheme.[15] Let Kraemer's list of "what Alfarabi calls the things all the people of the virtuous city ought to know in common" (113) provide the scheme:

(1) The First Cause and all that by which It is characterized.
(2) The things separate from matter and how each one of them is characterized by attributes specific to it; and the hierarchy of things separate from matter leading ultimately to the Active Intellect, and the activity of each.
(3) The heavenly substances and how each is characterized.

(4) The natural bodies below them; how they come into being and pass away; that what transpires among them does so by precision, mastery, providence (*'inaya: pronoia*), justice, and wisdom; and that there is no neglect, deficiency or injustice within them in any way.

(5) The generation (or: existence) of man; how the faculties of the soul originate; how the Active Intellect causes an illumination to emanate upon them so that the primary intelligibles are attained; volition (*irada: boulesis*) and choice (*ikhtiyar: proairesis*).

(6) The First Ruler and how revelation comes about.

(7) The rulers who must succeed him if he does not exist at some time.

(8) The city and its people and the happiness their souls attain; and the cities opposed to it and what their souls revert to after death: some to misery and some to non-existence.

(9) The virtuous nation and those that oppose it (114).

These realities are divided by Alfarabi into theoretical— (1) to (5)—and voluntary—(6) to (9). The theoretical components correspond with John of Damascene's outline in *De fide orthodoxa:*[16]

(1) Existence and nature of God: limitless and incomprehensible

(2) Creation: threefold division—invisible, visible, human being

(3) Angels: intellects with custody over earth and vision of God

(4) Visible creatures: heavens and four elements

(5) Paradise

(6) Creation of man "according to God's image": intellect and free will

Damascene emphasizes creation whereas Alfarabi presumes a necessary emanation, while Damascene's insistence that

"God does not belong to the existent beings, not because
He does not exist, but because He transcends all existent
beings and being itself" (Kraemer, 112) is not to be found
in Alfarabi. While he "stresses . . . the distinctiveness of the
deity from other existents, Alfarabi is not placing God
beyond being, but rather the First Cause, Primal Being (*al-
mawjud al-awwal*), the necessary existent and intellect *in
actu*" (114–15).

While this particular difference between John of
Damascene and Alfarabi will be of moment in a more detailed scrutiny of ways of formulating "the distinction," it
is noted here simply by way of contrast and not to suggest
any direct lineage between the works. In fact, as scholars
of the period note, there was a coincidence of interest and
of form among Jews, Muslims, and Christians "who refuted
philosophical opinions that destroyed the foundations of
their law" (107). This observation of Maimonides (in the
Guide 1.71) appears to follow Alfarabi's views of the
matter. Moreover, Kraemer maintains that there is a direct
link between Alfarabi and Rabbi Moses, contending that
"Maimonides conceived his role as that of Alfarabi's
philosopher-statesman . . . , whose function it was to posit
correct opinions for the virtuous city, or religious community" (109). His aims, then, in the *Foundations of the
Torah* will not be directly philosophical, but indirectly so,
as in *kalam* literature, where the "techniques, patterns and
themes . . . are aimed at the intellectual capacity of the
members of a community who cannot be addressed . . .
philosophically" (109).

Suffice it to note here that Kraemer has little difficulty
in finding the major themes of the theoretical part of
Alfarabi's design in the *Foundations of the Torah* (126–
32), and even more significantly, notes how Maimonides
refers to this treatment of his, in the *Guide* (3.35), as con-
taining "fundamental opinions" which the community
needs to pursue its goal. Alfarabi's "entire plan lays stress
upon the hierarchy of existence, the great chain of Being

suspended from the First, which should be represented for the people of the virtuous city by political symbols, i.e. the hierarchy of rulers and ruled; for the imitation of cosmic order is what induces political order and stability in the city" (135). Maimonides' treatment parallels this, with closer attention to the gift which singles out his people: the Torah. Yet withal "contemplation of the hierarchy of the beings and God's wisdom leads to love and fear of God and the desire to imitate his ways by righteous actions" (135).

Neither Alfarabi nor Maimonides had much use for *Kalam* when it had recourse to shoddy argument in defense of religion, yet neither felt such a task dispensable either (109). So it would not be implausible to find each engaged in a similar task when the needs of the community called for it. In that sense, one could propose the *Guide to the Perplexed* as a work of *Kalam* as well (108), through which "the apprehension of God, i.e. of his attributes that are His actions in the world, leads to political and ethical virtues" (141). This goal is stated explicitly in the final chapter of the *Guide* (3.54), showing once again how Maimonides' aims coincide with Alfarabi's in *The Virtuous City*, where "God's just and wise governance and ordering of the cosmos is the guiding and dominant theme" (141).

The cosmological scheme, then, so characteristic of the neoplatonic synthesis which characterized Arab philosophy, was shared by Jews and Christians in the same milieu. It offered a background within which to locate more detailed questions of observance regarding the Torah, and a way of attentuating the stark appearance of the revelation of the Qur'an, as well as offering a context for multiple decisions of *shar'ia*.[17] One may presume that philosophers like Ibn-Sina would themselves be more directly concerned with the *truth* of the scheme, especially as he will employ it to conjure a more purely intellectual union with God.[18] Yet it seems reasonable to think of it functioning within the community as Kraemer suggests: forming the set of background beliefs within which the real transactions between

God and humankind take place. Such is clearly the case for Dante's cosmology, which provides a cosmic setting for the journey whose moving forces are rather Virgil and Beatrice, as compassionate human understanding and the loving light of faith respectively, and whose terrain elaborates the human spirit far more than it imitates a cosmic order.

1.3 From Picturing the Connection to Articulating the Distinction

It is a neat question whether we *really* believe such background schemata which form the context for our lives of faith, or whether indeed such shaping presumptions may not offer a paradigm for our *real* beliefs.[19] Everything turns on the emphasis one gives to 'really', and whether that must mean 'explicitly', or whether one's implicit yet basic presumptions do not often function even more effectively than our more explicit beliefs to shape our outlook on the world. Some prefer 'convictions' to 'beliefs', as a way of discriminating among the ambiguities noted.[20] I have chosen to speak rather of 'picturing' or of a 'background scheme' to convey the role which the "great chain of being" played in Jewish, Christian and Muslim thought as well as in popular imagination. What pushed it farther into the background for Dante was undoubtedly Aquinas' explicit refusal to accord the scheme any analytic role in relating God to creation, so preparing the way for Galileo's dismantling it from our side. And Aquinas challenged the scheme precisely for obscuring the distinction—by pretending that anything created could share in the act of creation.[21]

The question had already been joined in Islam by al-Ghazali, who had ridiculed the scheme as lacking any warrant.[22] Yet his real target was the notion of emanation as such, which obscured the issues surrounding creation as a gracious act of God. For Maimonides, the intelligences

become angels who have a share in governance (as in John
of Damascene), but the scheme foundered for him when
considering God's knowledge of singulars (*Guide* 3.20).
The creator whom he knew from the Torah was directly
engaged with individuals; the One of the emanation scheme
only indirectly so as they are "ordered and defined." That
phrase is a favorite of Gersonides, writing in the century
after Aquinas, who located the source of Maimonides'
extreme agnosticism about divine attributes in this matter
of God's knowing individuals.[23] Gersonides' resolution,
however, beholden as it was to a literal rendering of the
scheme, failed to meet the issues involved; Maimonides
had the better instinct.

For, as Aquinas perceives clearly, the motivation for the
mediation scheme lay in the axiom: from One only one
can come. But that rule only governs natural emanations
(*per necessitatem naturae*), he insists, whereas "things proceed from God by way of knowledge and intellect, thus
allowing many to come forth immediately from a first
principle of divine simplicity" (*De pot.* 3.4). God's creation
may (and does) include diverse orders of being, but not in
such a way that one is created via another (*ST* 1.65.3.1).
The crucial reason why nothing created may share in the
act of creation—because that action consists in "producing
to be as such" (*ST* 1.45.5)—will be considered as we look
for ways to formulate "the distinction." What is at issue
here is a clean discrimination of creation from emanation,
of intentional activity from necessary bringing forth.

The scheme purported to serve an analytic purpose in
showing how many emanated from One; should it survive
after Aquinas' surgery, it will remain but one feature of a
contingent creation. And the point of that surgery was to
sever the Creator from intermediaries which would compromise the gratuity and intentionality of the very activity
which denominates God not as prime mover or first being,
but creator. So it is conceptual clarification of some moment that Aquinas is after.

The fact that the neoplatonic scheme allows one to conceive (and even to execute) a return to God—one thinks of Augustine's descriptions in Books 7 and 9 of the *Confessions*—does not authorize us, Aquinas insists, to let it obscure the way in which God's creative activity presupposes nothing at all. For it is one thing for a created order to assist in guiding intentional creatures to their proper end, yet quite another to let that fact and concern cloud the distinction between God and God's creation (*De pot.* 3.4.1). One thinks of the efforts of philosophers of religion to "construct" a divinity they can reach—and asks whether Aquinas has not touched a critical nerve extending from Ibn-Sina to our time.[24] There was something decidedly anthropomorphic in the way the emanation scheme so neatly replicated our ascent in knowing.

We have already noticed the ambiguity in Alfarabi's denominations: first cause, primal being, necessary existent. For what is first could be the first of many, and there are diverse ways of explicating 'necessary existent'. To be sure, he insists on the singularity of this *first*: it is uncaused, without beginning or end, it is not possible that this being not exist (I).[25] Indefinable because indivisible (IV), this being is distinguished from all other beings by that being by which it essentially exists: "it is one insofar as it possesses the being proper to it" (V); and in giving existence to others, it does not acquire any perfection beyond its proper perfection" for that "being which emanates from it to others is its essence (*dhat*) (VII). It would be difficult to realize a more explicit statement of divine oneness, yet Alfarabi is known to us more for the scheme of emanations which he elaborated than for these assertions. Moreover, one will have to await Ibn-Sina's explicit distinction of being (*wujud*) from essence (*dhat*) to appreciate how identifying them in the first being sets it off from everything else. Without Ibn-Sina's distinction, Alfarabi's assertions risk being taken as hyperbole, still imbedded in the context of the emanation scheme.

This factor alerts us to an endemic tendency we have in attempting to distinguish God from the world. We cannot help, it seems, treating this distinction as though it were one *in* the universe—like every other distinction we make.[26] And that tendency has two quite opposite effects. Taken in a Platonist (or Ash'arite) direction, it can result in denigrating the world we know, in favor of another (or a God) which *truly* is.[27] Or quite inversely, it will find congenial a system which seeks to comprehend the whole—including God—and so evacuate the original intent.[28] For if the distinction of God from the world is treated as one in the world, then either God will be exalted at the expense of God's world, or God will be seen as part of a necessary whole—since in each case the attempt is to understand the entirety: God-plus-world.

The clean alternative is simply to assert God to be *other than* the world, holding on quite firmly to the reality of the world in which we live. This can be considered Maimonides' position (as it is identified in our time with Karl Barth), but one always feels in such cases that one's religious self holds one's mind captive. For it takes but a little reflection to realize that God cannot be *that* neatly other if we are to use the name *creator,* or if divinity is to be in any way accessible to our discourse. If the first tendency fails in seeking global coherence, this tactic is internally incoherent for it undermines its founding assertion any time it uses the term 'God'.

What is needed, then, to articulate the distinction between God and the world in such a way as to respect the reality appropriate to each, is a distinction which makes its appearance, as it were, within the world as we know it, yet does not express a division within that world. Such a distinction would be of a logical type apt for articulating the relation of creator to creation: the connection which must display "the distinction." The conceptual materials came to the west in the form of Ibn-Sina's observation that existence (*wujud*) is not included in *what* we understand of things—their essence (or quiddity, *mahiyya*)—but can only be said to "happen to" them.[29] In Aquinas' hands this distinction will become the key to conceiving created beings in relation to their creator, as well as articulating what distinguishes the source of all that is from everything else which is, in short, "the distinction" we are in search of.

2. A Central Distinction: Essence/Existence

THE BACKGROUND SCHEME of Alfarabi offered an illusion of intelligibility useful for structuring social and political life in its image. It also provided human beings with a sense of their place in the cosmos, together with a way of attaining a vision of the whole. Ibn-Sina took it over wholesale, finding it especially useful in offering a psychological structure culminating in prophetic illumination—one of the cardinal tenets of Islam.[1] Yet it proved less helpful in explaining (as opposed to picturing) the emanation of many from One, and especially in distinguishing existence necessary in itself from that which is itself possible but made to be by another.[2]

This task will be far better served by his observation that the "nature which is proper to each thing (*haqiqa*: lit., its truth) is other than [its] existence (*al-wujud*), which is synonymous with affirming it to be the case (*al-ithbat*)."[3] This is the first clear formulation of a distinction between essence and existence, and it is this text of Avicenna's to which Aquinas has recourse in his early essay which has provided the framework for subsequent discussion in the West: *De ente et essentia*. Before considering the particularities of formulation, however, we should try to grasp the import of this conceptual tool—the better to appreciate why it often escapes philosophers' attention!

19

2.1 Significance of the Distinction

The stage has already been set: to respect the reality proper to creator and created alike, as well as to try to articulate the relation between them, i.e. creation, one needs a distinction which makes its appearance within the world as we know it yet does not express a division *within* that world. If we consider the references in Aristotle which can be considered part of the pre-history of the distinction of existence from essence, we will see that it is of the requisite sort. Aristotle's concern with definitions (in *Posterior Analytics*) led him to realize that "definition exhibits one single thing [vis., the essence], and that what human nature is and the fact that man exists are not the same thing" (92b8). And they are not the same thing since they answer two different questions: what is it? and is it? (Note that "is it?" easily moves from the purely existential question: "are there really unicorns?" to the question for a judgment of truth: "is it the case that . . .?" Aristotle, with his realist temperament, often conflated the two, hence Ibn-Sina's observation "existence is synonymous with affirmation.")

Yet the question which structures inquiry is not the factual one but the essential one: what is it? So the existential question is easily elided, or simply presupposed. And so it was for Aristotle, who could presume the world as an eternally given context—so much so that he simply assumed the validity of universal instantiation in logic, never imagining, as it were, empty classes.[4] Yet it is that same presumption regarding existence which Maimonides found calloused (and certainly revealingly pagan) in Aristotle's disregard for God's providential care for individuals: "He holds that God, may He be exalted, takes care of the spheres and of what is in them. . . . Alexander has formulated this, saying that in Aristotle's opinion God's providence ends at the sphere of the moon" (*Guide* 3.17).[5] Maimonides' reaction pinpoints the issue: how to *characterize* individual life—which is ostensibly of greatest value and yet so vulnerable to extinction? Moreover, if Aristotle meant to rescue the primary reality of the individual existing thing from the endemic predilection of scientific inquiry for essential structures, one could argue that the attempt to find the proper characterization of existence represents his finest instincts.[6]

2.1.1 THE EXISTENTIAL QUESTION

We have already noted how the question arises for us: bereft of the background tapestry of the great chain of being, how can we sustain our conviction that life—especially human life with its attendant relationships—is what is most precious, when it is also most vulnerable? (Structures perdure; individuals come and go.) Once that intricately woven scheme has been shown to offer illusory confidence, the question still remains, though now posed in a more starkly analytic mode: how can one hope to formulate what our ordinary ways of knowing must take for granted —the fact of existence? For existence does not mark a division within our world so much as something which *happens* within it, as when a baby is born. What before was not is now present in our midst, yet population statistics are merely increased by one. The ironies which strike us when these perspectives cross have spawned a philosophical movement—existentialism—and give body to what we can recognize to be a great literature.[7] To my mind, what is significant is that the ironies *do* strike us, overwhelmingly at times, and that we can readily discriminate great litera-ture from trite or formulaic imitations by its singular capacity to render the individual present to us. But where can one go from here?

One may, in the context of this inquiry, go on to recog-nize that this is the very distinction we were looking for: one which makes its appearance in our world yet does not distinguish *kinds* within it. Then it would also be part of the grammar of the matter that the "fact of existence" did not name a kind within the world, or as it has often been put: 'existence' is not a predicate.[8] So we would be prepared to acknowledge our inability to formulate the "fact of existence" since formulations are reserved for kinds; and by the same token realize why philosophers may overlook what everyone can recognize, since their business is formulation.

2.1.2   RELATING TO ALL THAT IS

The fact that existence escapes direct formulation, moreover, suggests another way in which distinguishing *to be* from *what* something is may assist us in elucidating the transcendence of that One whose essence is simply to be: the Creator. Yet before scrutinizing *that* formula—inchoately Ibn-Sina's and explicitly Aquinas'—one strategy for illuminating what we mean by existence may be suggested. It is grounded in my phrase for what we find most precious: human life with its attendant relationships. For it is one thing to describe unicorns, yet quite another to relate to one. The human spirit, it is true, can enter into many sorts of relationships, one of which is knowing or describing something, yet the sense in which human relationships are treasured is one which presupposes the reality of each of those relating. One trying to entertain the same sort of relationship with a fictional character would be deluded, yet the fictional character is not an illusion. Our manner of relating, then, to the existing world reveals the grasp we have of what escapes our formulation—namely, existence.

This manner of relating is often conveyed by the term 'attitude'. Customarily lean in conceptual force, we can pass off attitudes as ephemeral, yet the term is rich in metaphorical allusion. If we think of *attitude* in one of its senses, as the pitch of a plane's wing designed to maximize lift, we might be led to reflect on our characteristic ways of approaching the world. So endemic that they coalesce into our character, they become the very thing which we are so close to as to be virtually unable to change. As one writer has put it, were we so inclined to self-improvement as to make a list of all the things in our life—our overt relationships as well as our possessions—with the goal of examining each for its merit, and were we so efficient as to effect a complete list, one element would inevitably be lacking: namely, our relationship to all the things in our life.[9] And were some power able to alter *that*, then our relationship to each of the items would be altered *tout d'un coup*. Such is normally called *conversion*, and justly regarded to be beyond our own power to execute.

This capacity, moreover, to relate (potentially) to all there is, is what defined mind for the medievals—intellect and will—as a spiritual power. *Spirit* referred not in the first instance to an unfamiliar mode of existence, but to a capacity for relating on different levels and across the space-time parameters endemic to bodies. Hence Kierkegaard, in his pseudonymous treatise on the self (*Sickness unto Death*) characterizes the self as spirit, that is, a *relating*.[10] Nor was he innocent, in his choice, of the theological elaborations—east and west—of the mystery of the triune God via "subsistent relations." For relation remains the most elusive of Aristotle's categories, not properly an accident for its being is not *in* but *ad*; which is to say that it does not exist *in* another so much as "between" the *relata*. Medievals, to be sure, tried to minimize the ontological scandal by focusing on the qualities of the subjects so related, so finding *accidental* correlates for particular relations. And that is of course the case: to be differently related is to become a different person in recognizable respects. Yet relating cannot be translated into those changes without remainder.

It is this attitude towards the world, then, which may be called our "sense of reality," which expresses the grasp we have of existence. It is what artists can both convey and elicit from us through their work, and what a novelist like Tolstoy delineates so finely in his characters. Our tendency

to want to explicate such a complex of attitudes "psycho-
logically" only displays the predilection we have to find a
structural (or essential) explanation for everything—including what escapes that formulation, existence. Or if our
psychological explanations follow the natural contours of
their subject sufficiently to escape reductive (causal)
schemes, we will be drawn through them to a set of descriptions which express in a more analytic fashion basic human
attitudes towards existence.[11]

All of this is presented to show us how we might find
analogues for a distinction that must be strictly inexpressible, in those equally mysterious attitudes we find ourselves
assuming in the face of reality. If this level of articulating
"the distinction" is to be in the service of knowing an
unknowable God, we had best remind ourselves that the
traditional analogue for divinity—the human creature—is
also quite unknown to us. Were we to presume to begin
with a self we understood, and wonder how divinity sur-
passed our understanding, we would be off on a false start.
Yet here too, all is not mysterious, for the progressive
consciousness we can gain of our characteristic attitudes to
the world can offer us some insight into that self which is
its microcosm, and whose "sense of reality" expresses—in
whatever we do or think—our grasp of that inexpressible
dimension of the world which is its reality.

2.2 Distinguishing the Creator from Creation

The term often translated 'reality' in Arabic philosophical and religious writings is *haqiqa,* the substantive for
haqq: true, genuine, authentic—or real.[12] What is most
true, then, will be what truly exists, and what so exists will
have its *raison d'etre* from within itself rather than without.
So much so, indeed, that Ibn-Sina finds in "the necessary
existent" the very paradigm of *al-haqiqa.* For it is what is
"true (real) in itself, always, while the possible existent is

true (real) by another, and false in itself. Indeed, whatever is other than the necessary existent—itself unique—is false in itself."[13] Moreover, these strong words follow from the initial definition given of *al-haqiqa,* which offers three consecutive meanings: (1) existence *in re* absolutely, (2) perpetual existence, (3) state of mind designating a state of affairs when the one renders the other adequately, as in 'true affirmation' or 'true conviction'.[14]

From these passages, then and others as well (8.3, 8.6), one would rightly construe Ibn-Sina's orientation to be existential: what is true is, in the first instance, what really exists.[15] That orientation will become even more significant as we come to appreciate the thoroughly "essentialist" character of his thought.[16] Moreover, we would not be amiss in construing that orientation as an effort to secure the difference of the necessary existent from everything emanating from it, in the face of the inherited scheme of essential orders of being which tended to obscure that fact, designed as it was to attenuate the scandal of many originating from one. And this effort reflected religious concerns as well, for emanation could be assimilated to creation only by radically contrasting possible with necessary being.

And the contrast is engineered by virtue of distinguishing quiddity from existence in everything other than the necessary existent:

> it is evident that for everything there is a proper nature (*haqiqa*: truth, reality) which is its quiddity. And we know that the nature (*haqiqa*) proper to each thing is other than its existence (*al-wujud*), which is synonymous with its affirmation.[17]

The reason follows our mode of understanding:

> if you say: 'the nature (*haqiqa*) of this thing exists'—concretely, in the mind, or absolutely (which contains the other two modes)—that will require an *intention* understood to be acquired.[18]

In other words, to say 'this nature is this nature' or even 'this nature is a thing' would be tautologous, but not so to affirm that it exists.

As if to corroborate the suspicion that this distinction is at the service of setting off the first existent from everything which flows from it, Ibn-Sina nowhere analyzes *al-wujud* as distinct from the nature (or quiddity), but uses the difference noted to conclude that "the First has no quiddity other than its [to-be] (*al-anniyya*)."[19] And the reason for denying quiddity to what necessarily exists stems from his manner of conceiving existence as "coming to" the nature. So he must ward off a conception of necessary existence as something *attributed to* the necessary existent. What we must rather say is that "there is no quiddity for the necessary existent other than the fact that it is the necessary existent; and this is its [to be]."[20]

One senses a formal cast to all this, displayed above all in the supporting reasoning, but betrayed also by the absence of any direct treatment of *al-wujud*: existence. As what alone, and thus uniquely characterizes the First and Necessary existent, it cannot fail to merit a special dignity, yet the most we can say of it is that it "comes to" (*advenit, accidit*) the essence (or quiddity). Hence the charge (notably by Averroes) that Ibn-Sina blundered in presenting existence as an accident.[21] The charge distorts Ibn-Sina's treatment of the distinction, yet he leaves himself open to it by offering no alternative way of conceiving the matter. Anawati has characteristically pinpointed the reason: "because he begins with essence, Avicenna is brought inevitably to consider the *esse* which affects it as an accident."[22] The very formal character of his thought leaves him no alternative way of putting things.

Maimonides will gratefully adopt the distinction as a way of expressing the transcendence of God, presenting the matter in phrases encapsulating Ibn-Sina:

> It is known that existence is . . . something that is superadded to the quiddity of what exists. This is clear and necessary with regard to everything the existence of

which has a cause. . . . As for that which has no cause
for its existence, there is only God, may He be magni-
fied and glorified, who is like that...—that His existence
is necessary. Accordingly, His existence is identical with
His essence and His true reality, and His essence is His
existence. (*Guide* 1.57)

He will play upon the received understanding of Ibn-Sina
that "existence is an accident attaching to what exists"
(ibid.) to reinforce his standing contention that we can
make no positive attributions regarding divinity, aligning
'exists' with the three attributes of God accepted as
essential:

Consequently He exists, but not through an existence
other than His essence; and similarly He lives, but not
through life; He is powerful, but not through power;
He knows, but not through knowledge (ibid.).

As for Ibn-Sina, this manner of putting things also rein-
forces *tawhid*: the central faith affirmation that God alone
is one:

To ascribe to Him—whose existence is necessary, who is
truly simple, to whom composition cannot attach in any
way—the accident of oneness is . . . absurd. . . . He is one
not through oneness (ibid.).

So for Maimonides, as for Ibn-Sina, the distinction of
existence from essence functions primarily to distinguish
possible from necessary being, and as a way of affirming
the uniqueness of the necessary existent. It does not, in
their hands, allow us to say anything more about divinity
than that, nor do they use it to delineate the *sui-generis*
activity of creating.[23] These steps will be taken by Aquinas.

2.3   Refining the Distinction

Aquinas' early essay, *De ente et essentia* (On Being
and Essence) has been expertly researched and amply
commented upon.[24] It stands out for the way it neatly

finds a path through the conflicting interpretations he faced, as well as for its undergirding of his subsequent development of the matter. We shall be concerned with the work itself as it moves the distinction beyond Ibn-Sina's initial formulations, and toward subsequent development of existence as *actus essendi* (the act of being). For it will be this latter formulation which offers a way of characterizing divinity, and of delineating the properly divine activity of creation.

What is more, for Aquinas the two will be related: a characterization of divinity as that One whose essence is simply to-be will allow him to delineate creation as "producing to-be as such" (*ST* 1.45.5). So clarifying the distinction will help us formulate the connection. And there is reason to suspect that Ibn-Sina was dispensed from refining the distinction because the emanation scheme offered so handy a way of picturing the connection. What fuels that suspicion is his third way of considering natures: namely, "in an absolute manner, which contains the other two."[25] How can we say that such "things" exist (as his proof demands we do) when we are asked to consider them "absolutely"—that is, prescinding from any mode of existing? Here is where some locate the tension between Aristotle and Plato embodied in the emanation scheme which Ibn-Sina took over from Alfarabi.[26]

Despite his insistence that quiddity, in and of itself, is *not*, it remains that existence is conceived relative to essences—as what "happens to" them.[27] So the primacy he accords to essence will allow him to introduce those "absolute natures," which one cannot precisely identify with the intelligences of Alfarabi's scheme, but which one would naturally conceive by analogy with them. Moreover, it is these essences, taken absolutely, which Gilson sees as providing the objects of knowledge which would constitute a crucial point of departure for the conceptual realism of a Duns Scotus.[28] In any case, the theory of knowledge developed by Avicenna (and profoundly influential in the Middle Ages) could dispense with abstraction, properly so-called, for an intellect so illuminated by the "agent intelligence" as to be able to *receive* such essential forms.[29] In this way realism was secured.

But such an explanation of knowing by way of a purely passive intellect jeopardizes the activity proper to secondary causes. For if knowing, the highest human activity, involves neither abstraction nor judgment, then a scenario in which the first cause gives creatures a capacity for acting is threatened. If we identify such a scenario with creation, properly so-called, then the Avicennian alternative is certainly more consonant with an emanationist view. Where the triad— emanation, essence, reception—characterizes the legacy of Avicenna, that of creation, *esse*, judgment will mark the specific achievement of Aquinas.[30] How is it that he negotiates this difference?

Philosophical breakthroughs depend in part on one's initial perspectives, in part on the conceptual tools available, yet finally on one's ability to put them to work. We have already noted Anawati's observation regarding Ibn-Sina's starting point: essences. He goes on to note how "St. Thomas began from the existing thing and made *esse* what is most intimate and profound in this thing (*ST* 1.8.1.4). The relation of *esse* to essence is not the rapport of two entities of the same order—of an accident to a substance— even from a logical viewpoint, but the relation of act to potency."[31] It should be clear, then, that the two viewpoints are entirely different.[32] Beginning with the existing individual already insinuates that the primacy should go to existence (in the spirit of Aristotle), and reduplicating the act/potency distinction offers a neat formulation for that primacy.

Here we have the achievement of *De ente et essentia*: the iterated analogy—matter : form :: essence : esse :: potency : act. And by clarifying that the first couplet (matter + form) is what constitutes the essence of composite creatures, Aquinas could indicate—via the next couplet—that *esse* would bear an intelligibility with respect to essence analogous to that which form conveys to matter.

But only *analogous,* and in fact it will be a "surplus intelligibility" quite beyond our conception—indeed, of the elusive sort I have already suggested (§2.1.2). For the commensurate object of human understanding remains the "quiddity or nature existing in a material body" (*ST* 1.84.7), just as the primary candidate for substance is the individual existing thing.

Aquinas does not, in other words, take the protomystical step of questioning the reality of the created essence, even though it be *conceived* in potency to *esse*. What exists is the subject, and the subject has being by its essence. To say that the essence bears a relation to existence of potency to act does not entail that it is itself, as it were, in potency to non-being. For the test case of spiritual substances, without the disintegrating factor of material composition, there is no potency whatsoever to non-being.[33] In fact, Aquinas specifies, "there is no such tendency in the whole of created nature, by which it is possible for something to tend towards nothingness," for even in the corruption of material things the matter remains and the form is reduced to something potential (*De pot.* 5.3.).

These specifications, in the last case aimed explicitly at Avicenna, are clearly designed to secure the reality of individual things—Aquinas' starting point. They indicate how we are to understand the analogies drawn in *De ente,* and how gingerly we are to endeavor to grasp *esse*. We cannot cede to the temptation to denigrate created things to exalt their creator. For it amounts to an even greater praise to affirm a creator able to constitute creatures to function as agents in their own right, having existence as a gift, to be sure, but *de jure,* as it were.[34] In fact, Aquinas never employs *esse* as a specific perfection, and always considers essence the principle of intelligibility.[35] The intelligibility proper to *esse* must remain metaphorical, as a sign of the transcendence of the relation which it helps to formulate: that of creator to creature.

The metaphors are two—the first taken directly from the root analogy of potency to act: *actus essendi* act of being); the second reminiscent of the emanation scheme: participation (*ens per essentiam/per participationem*).[36] A summary text employs them both:

> *Esse* (to-be) itself is the ultimate act in which everything can participate while it itself participates in nothing. Whence we say: if there be anything which is subsistent *esse* itself—as we say God is—then that one participates in nothing at all. Other subsistent forms, however, must participate in *esse* as potency to act, so given that they are to this extent in potency, they can participate in something else (*Q.D. De anima* 1.6.2).

The being which is subsistent in divinity is to be construed, then, as though it were an act, and furthermore an act in which created things—even spiritual creatures—participate as "having *esse* rather than being their own to-be" (1.3.4). Such is in fact the "definition" of *participation,* if it can be called that. For little, except the form of predication itself, can tell us what it is to "have being," and the contrast term—to be one's own to-be—reaches utterly beyond our ken.[37]

The most fruitful strategy, I would suggest, is to return to the triad which Gilson calls to our attention—creation-*esse*-judgment—in the context of safeguarding the agency proper to created things (or secondary causes). We know how contested an issue this was in Islamic thought, so much so that even to broach it here would carry us too far afield. (Maimonides summarizes the positions nicely in his mini-commentary on Job [*Guide,* 3.22-23]). What is pertinent here is Aquinas' choice of *act* to render *esse* intelligible to us. It is my contention that the act of understanding, and in particular the act of *judgment,* provides the rationale for this analogy.[38] For it is through the judgment of truth that we attain to what is the case, when we assert things in fact to be such-and-such. This focus on the activity of judgment allows him to unit the different senses which Ibn-Sina found in *haqiqa*—True, authentic, real—by insisting that it is not "adequation" but

the *judgment* of adequation which yields a true statement.[39] Truth, then, is not a property of things or of
propositions, but results from an activity called judging; a
second-order activity in the realm of knowing which com-
pletes the inquiry by ascertaining whether what we maintain
is in fact the case.

Truth, in other words, does not "come to" statements
any more than existence "comes to" natures; but represents
their culmination as asserted by a responsible knower,
much as *esse* expresses a thing's coming into existence by
the creative power of a gracious God. True propositions
are neither found nor do they emanate from a primal set
of axioms; they must be asserted by one able to offer suit-
able warrant on their behalf. Similarly, individual existing
things are not mere givens nor emergent phenomena; they
come about as a result of an act on the part of the one
whose nature is simply to-be, and hence must be said to be
"pure act" (*ST* 1.3.2), whereby such things may be said to
have (or to participate in) *esse*.

These last statements will not be argued here. They are
presented by way of conceptual clarification: how it is
that Aquinas conceived *esse* on the analogy of an activity.
It is not, of course, the activity of a subject any more than
it is an accident of a substance, for *actiones sunt suppositi*
(actions are proper to already subsisting things). Yet it is
best conceived on the analogy of action, particularly of
that activity imminent to subjects called *knowing,* and
most particularly of its culmination in judgment.[40] What is
more, this activity is not to be misconceived as the passive
reception of a divine illumination, but as what we experience it to be: that activity whereby we assume a definite
attitude towards the world, affirming what we state to be
the case. That capacity, then, so to relate oneself to existence, becomes our paradigm for understanding existence—
not as something "coming to" a nature, but as that nature's
graciously being made present. It remains but to show how
this paradigm also offers us a way of formulating the first
member of the triad: creation.

2.4 Formulating the Action/Relation Which Is Creation

It would be difficult to find a more explicit and forth-right delineation of creation than Ibn-Sina's:

> This is what it means that a thing is created, that is, receiving its existence from another. . . . As a result everything, in relation to the first cause, is created. . . . Therefore, every single thing, except the primal One, exists after not having existed with respect to itself.[41]

Yet this assertion is considerably attenuated—perhaps in deference to Aristotle's teaching on the eternity of matter —by Ibn-Sina's discussion of the possibility to exist which must accompany something's "not having existed with respect to itself." That "possibility to exist must be . . . an existing *intention* [which], relative to thing-to-exist . . . finds its subject in *matter*."[42] That something may exist is then a real possibility in the world, taking the form of an "intentional" qualification of *matter*.

Again, one finds Ibn-Sina's "essentialism" overriding his grasp of the difference between what we can say of something (*haqiqa*) and its existence (*al-wujud*). Aquinas insists, more in the spirit of that distinction, that the *possibility* at issue here is logical rather than real—that asserting that something might exist (before it existed) would not yield a contradiction.[43] If there be question of an active potency, that will properly be found "in the power of the agent [God] rather than in any passive potentiality of matter" (*De pot.* 3.1.2). And that power stems from the fact that "God alone is simply to-be" (*ST* 1.45.5.1), so that "the primary effect [of God's agency] is to-be itself, which is presupposed to all other effects but itself presupposes no other effect; whence it follows that to grant *esse* as such is the effect proper to the first cause alone, according to the power inherent in it" (*De pot.* 3.4).

We have already seen (§1.3) how this insistence on Aquinas' part effectively dismantled the revered scheme of emanation, rendering it at once incoherent and pointless.

For if nothing *can* share in the creative act, then it is silly to have an array of pretenders. The role it is playing here is to elucidate the analytic power of the distinction between essence and existence. For outside of the original essay *De ente et essentia,* that distinction has no explicit role to play in Aquinas' thought except to secure proper discourse concerning divinity (including the relation of God's eternal action with events in time) and to elucidate the relation of creation. Once that is established, Aquinas will proceed to consider things in their essential natures. That is why Josef Pieper spoke of creation as "the hidden element in the philosophy of St. Thomas"—everywhere present yet all the while presupposed.[44]

What *is* present in things, however, is a real relation to the creator—"already alluded to in the term 'creature'" (*De pot.* 3.3)—which is displayed in the ontological unity possessed by each being by the fact of its existence.[45] For the relation of potency to act is precisely such that no third element is required to effect the unity of existence. Here we have the reason why Aquinas refuses to admit any potency to non-being in existing things beyond the propensity of matter to disintegration. For the essence actualized possesses the integrity of its proper *act.* From that ontological consistency flow the actions proper to subsisting agents—so much their own, indeed, as to be ab le, in that higher order of existence proper to grace, even to *merit* what their savior promised: eternal life. It is this real relation to the One, really present in each existing thing in its ontological constitution by essence and existence (as potency to act), and exhibited in a doctrine of human acts whereby one stands responsibly before God, that Aquinas' recasting of Avicenna's distinction of existence from essence (as something happening to it) finds its proper vindication. Moreover, the analogy of potency to act renders explicit Aquinas' starting point as well: the existential unity of the existing individual.

3. The Nature of Divinity

HOW TO CONCEIVE THE nature of divinity? It must, for us, be considered in relation to what we know—the world—and yet *shown* in that very consideration not to be part of the world. This is the logical demand following upon the meaning of the term 'God' as Aquinas introduces it: "the beginning and end of all things, and of rational creatures especially" (*ST* 1.2 Intro.). This descriptive definition has the advantage of capturing what is common to the three traditions we are considering, by reminding us that the *principium* (beginning) is not contained in the set of all things. Here is "the distinction" for which we have been seeking a proper formulation.

3.1 The Role Aquinas' Distinction Plays in this Inquiry

The candidate proposed—the distinction between essence and existence—finds its roots in Alfarabi, its first articulation in Ibn-Sina, is approved by Maimonides, and brought to a refined status by Aquinas. What Aquinas clarifies is the logical (or categorical) status of this distinction. By transforming existence from "something which happens to" an essence to that to which essence must be related as the primary ontological constituent of an existing thing,

Aquinas proposed reshuffling the metaphysical schemata inherited from Aristotle and Plato through the Arabs.

For those schemes concurred in relating matter to form as the constituents intrinsic to essence, yet beyond that point they diverged considerably. The intention of Plotinus that the One lay "beyond being" reflected Plato's similarly pregnant remarks in the *Republic* of the good beyond being.[1] Aristotle also noted that the queries 'what is it?' and 'is it?' were irreducible one to another. Yet the penchant of scientific inquiries to answer the first invariably gave preference to essence over the "mere fact" of something's being present. Indeed, as we shall see, that remains the endemic tendency of philosophical inquiry as well.

It is not as though Aquinas worked a revolution to which all subsequent philosophers had to acquiesce—in the manner of Plato and Aristotle, and to a lesser extent, Kant. His proposal is rather like a call to a personal conversion, which one may more easily ignore. That conversion may be described from his starting point: existing beings rather than essences (Anawati); or from his method: as a return to the subject who knows and makes judgments concerning existing beings (Lonergan).[2] I shall attempt in this chapter to show how that call to conversion, as embodied and displayed in the distinction of essence from *esse,* offers a fresh way of conceiving the nature of divinity.

What is fresh about it, as we shall see, is the way it invites one to transcend one's normal patterns of inquiry, which are tied to answering 'what is it?', to try to locate the answer to that question (the essence) in a subordinate relationship to something else: the act of existing. In short, we are asked to remind ourselves that essences, properties, and the like, cannot be the term of our philosophical inquiry, since they must be considered not things but constituents of things. It should be clear how this invitation moves one in a resolutely Aristotelian direction, confirming the individual existing thing to be the paradigm instance of *what is*: substance.

What may not be so immediately clear is how uncongenial such an invitation will appear to philosophers. For whether they conceive their business as systematic elaboration or conceptual clarification, it is essences they are after, as answering 'what is that, anyway?' In that respect, then, it should not be surprising to find most philosophers either vaguely "Platonist" in their orientation (in the common or vulgar sense of that term); or in adamant opposition to such an orientation, and so more or less answering to a "positivist" description. Aquinas' distinction offers a response rather than a reaction to the endemic "Platonism" by taking as its starting point (and resolution) the individual existing thing; and by presenting the answer to the question 'what is it?' as the penultimate rather than the final response to the original *elan* of the inquiry.

For if essence is in potency to an act of existing, then *what* can be said about a thing will be subordinate to something else: the act of judgment—or, in more colloquial speech, *how* it is said, or the manner in which what is said is put forth. Following this lead, we will forebear asking *whether* our concepts apply to the subject in question, but rather ask *how* they might be used to elucidate it. And if that be true of things in the world, it must *a fortiori* be the case when considering divinity.

Here we have the connection between this central distinction of Aquinas and his attention to analogy, notably in discourse about God. And once that connection is seen, one would be less surprised to find an "Aquinas who looks more like Wittgenstein than Avicenna."[3] In fact, the reflections of the later Wittgenstein on the multiple uses to which *we* put language will appear as serendipitous confirmations of the role which Aquinas' distinction plays in our attentiveness to language and the ways we use language.

Nor would it be surprising following what we have noticed, were philosophers to vary widely in heeding Wittgenstein's admonitions regarding the multiple uses of language. One may indeed, with the help of Gilson's three classic essays, trace a lineage through medieval platonism from Avicenna to Duns Scotus, which secured conceptual realism by a theory of knowledge and a philosophical method which presumed our formulations to be congruent with the essences of things.[4] No second thoughts here about *how* we might use the languages and concepts available to us; with clear formulation went simple application. Yet what gave such a movement confidence, it seems, was Avicenna's conviction about natures taken "absolutely"— a position formally compatible with his distinction of existence from the nature of things, yet potentially in tension with it.

The import of Aquinas' distinction, then, reveals itself in the very way in which one pursues a philosophical inquiry. Here I shall illustrate how it may be used to structure consideration of the divine nature. In chapter four we shall extend that inquiry to the classical question of divine attributes. The two inquiries are intimately connected, of course, as natures reveal themselves through their characteristic properties, yet especially so *in divinis,* where the primary distinguishing feature of divinity—simpleness—seems to militate against any attribution whatsoever. So this chapter must concentrate on that feature—its religious roots and motivations, as well as the other "formal features" attendant upon it: perfection, unchangeableness, limitlessness, and oneness—before being able to show how these austere parameters will affect how we may attribute more engaging things of God.[5]

3.2   No Composition in the First Being

We may ease into the complexities aroused by asserting simpleness by pondering the apparently straightforward question: does God have a nature? First of all, the very form of the question is either deliberately arresting or misleading. It would be deliberately arresting were it posed in the spirit of our existentialist who wished to show how human being was distinguished from every other existent by asking: does *man* have a nature? It would be misleading if one emphasized the verb 'have' so as to presume that God were an individual partaking of a divine nature, thus losing sight of the *de jure* identification of name with common noun in 'God': what Jew, Christian, and Muslim incorporate in their initial act of faith.[6]

We have seen how Ibn-Sina reacted to what the question implies by insisting that "the first has no quiddity," since his observation that "the nature proper to each thing is other than its existence" (1.5, 31:12) led him to conclude that "whatever has a quiddity is caused." (Ibn-Sina clearly introduced the essence/existence distinction at the service of the yet more basic distinction between "the first" and all that emanates therefrom.) So he eschews a parallel line of inquiry concerning divinity, as though this special quiddity might be the "sort to which necessarily existing were added," finding such a formulation incoherent. For what exists necessarily cannot be conceived as having existence "happen to it," but must rather find "its subsistence realized in itself." As a result, "there is no quiddity for the necessary existent other than the fact that it is necessary existent—and that is its to-be (*al-anniyya*)."[7]

Ibn-Sina is blazing the trail which Aquinas will more clearly trace, by crafting a philosophical distinction to mutually elucidate (1) a religious conviction: the uniqueness of God (*tawhid*), and (2) a standing philosophical notion: necessary existent. Alfarabi had accumulated the assertions: being without cause, it is not possible that the first being not exist. Moreover, it must then exist without matter and not in a subject, but be *one* simply by possessing the being proper to it; and "that being which emanates from it to others is its essence (*dhat*)."[8] What Ibn-Sina specified is that ordinary considerations of the natures (*haqiqa*) of things reveals a quiddity (*mahiyya*) distinct from existence (*al-wujud*). What then distinguishes divinity from everything emanating from it is the fact that its essence (*dhat* = answer to question: what is it?) is simply existence.

So asked whether God has a nature, Ibn-Sina was inclined to answer *no*: there is no quiddity in God. For that is what the form of the question presupposes: what is that basic feature (distinct from existing) whereby God is divine? Yet not wishing to rule the question: what is God? out of court, he qualified the *no*: there is no quiddity other than its to-be. And since that response is expressly paradoxical, in his own terms, a just summary statement of his position would say: for Ibn-Sina, God has no quiddity. But God's essence (*dhat*) is existing—and this is intended as a formulation of necessary existence.[9]

Alfarabi had already insisted that the first being's "lacking any cause at all for its existence" meant that it could not be composed of parts—lest these be construed as (formal) causes of its being what it is. And being indivisible, it must be "one in respect of the necessary existence proper to it."[10] It is a crucial conceptual step to note explicitly, as Ibn-Sina did, that this "necessary existence" is not a feature of divinity but identified with its essence. For that explication secures the affirmation of *unity* which Alfarabi intended. And Maimonides will profit by Ibn-Sina's distinction, as well, to articulate the central affirmation of the *Guide* (and of the Torah) that God is inherently one. These distinctions allow one to see how absurd it would be "to ascribe [the accident of oneness] to Him whose existence is necessary, who is truly simple, to whom composition cannot attach in any way; . . . He is not one through oneness"(1.57).

The motivation for denying composition in God should be clear from these Muslim and Jewish antecedents and interlocutors with Aquinas.[11] It responds to a combined philosophical and religious pressure: what is necessary in the sense of uncaused excludes component (formal) causes or a composing (efficient) cause; what is God alone with

no other god alongside must be set off from everything
else that is by being indivisible and so undefinable. Yet it is
one thing to deny composition and another to find the
proper terms in which to affirm oneness. Ibn-Sina took the
initial step in this direction by first distinguishing existence
from essences, and then identifying God's essence with
existence. That formal assertion assured divinity a transcendent unity by denying of it that mode of composition
inherent to every existing thing.

Yet Ibn-Sina's brilliant formulation was unable to *show*
how this lack of composition meant a perfection in divinity, because he was unclear what ontological place to assign
to *existence*. Nor is the worry an idle one, for (as Aquinas
notes) lack of composition would seem to be a defect since
we normally rank orders of being by degrees of differentiation: *distinguer pour unir*.[12] And lest one think this a mere
lapse on the part of those who fail to distinguish intentional from material realities, one can find sophisticated
treatments of the divine nature quite baffled by assertions
of simpleness.[13]

So lest such assertions be tarred by association with an
outmoded (and unfounded) set of Greek predilections, or
challenged as incongruent with accepted treatments of
essences-*cum*-properties, one needs to be able to show how
simpleness amounts to a perfection when claimed as a formal feature of divinity. In short, one needs the conceptual
tools to display God's simpleness as something other than
undifferentiation. The point of asserting simpleness in
divinity must be more than insisting "that no distinctions
can be made in God;" in fact, this assertion will have to be
compatible with many distinctions in God: knowing, willing, and the like.[14] How, then, can we understand God's
simpleness not as a lack in God but as formulating that
perfection expressed religiously by Jew, Christian, and
Muslim: God is one?

3.3   Affirming God's Simpleness

Simpleness would not be a defect, but rather a way of distinguishing divinity from all else that is, as well as linking all that exists with God, if that which God is said simply to-be were itself the sum total of all perfections. But this is precisely what Aquinas insists, in showing that the essence of divinity can be none other than to-be: "*esse* (to-be) is the actuality of all acts, and therefore the perfection of all perfections" (*De pot.* 7.2.9). This is what he is enabled to say after having shown in *De ente et essentia* how all existing things, even immaterial ones, can be said to be composed—by a mode of composition one step higher than that of matter to form: essence to *esse*. For once we begin to consider existence as the act proper to essence, then we can link it with perfection.

3.3.1   FINDING LOGICAL SPACE FOR *ESSE*

His argument deserves scrutiny, however, for it does invite us to consider things in a fresh light—and unless we do so his remarks about *esse* may sound extravagant.[15]

> For we should not think of anything added to what I call *esse* as though it were yet more "formal" than *esse,* determining it as act determines potency.... For nothing can be added to *esse* which is extrinsic to it, but non-being. . . . Therefore *esse* is not determined by another as potency is by act, but rather as act is [limited] by potency. . . . And so this *esse* is distinguished from another *esse* insofar as it is of such and such a nature (*De pot.* 7.2.9).

The example he gives of act being determined by potency is that of the "soul [which] is the act of organized physical body." In the context of a continuing dialogue with Avicenna, this example is especially significant, for

Avicenna took exception to Aristotle on the soul's being
the form of a material body. He preferred to identify what
makes us human with the soul itself, even if a soul became
individual only after having been in a body.[16]

Aquinas gives this argument in an extended treatment of
God's simpleness, and particularly of his culminating formulation of simpleness: that "in God substance or essence
is the same as to-be." The objector puts what might well
be our question: what is so great about predicating *esse* of
God? For just as prime matter must be determined by
forms, so *esse* must be determined by all the proper predi-
caments—what's so perfect about that? We may not put
the question in terms of "prime matter," but ours would
have the same thrust: if the fact of something's existing is
normally presupposed to inquiry, and we are always concerned with what something is, with ascertaining its properties, how all of a sudden can what everyone presupposes
be elevated *above* the object of our investigations? And if
our query be something like that, we should recognize
ourselves more akin to Ibn-Sina than to Aquinas: existence
may well be distinct from essence (by the arguments he
gives), yet we quite naturally think of it as "something
happening to" essence.

Yet, as Anawati remarked, Aquinas begins not with
essences but with existing things, which Aristotle insisted
were the paradigm instances of substance. And when we
consider existing things, the *actual* quality of existence
may begin to dawn upon us, or at least we may begin to be
struck by the ironies attendant upon *always* subordinating
individuals to their formal structures. The nice question
of Aristotle has always been: if the individual offers the
paradigm for substance, can we say more of an individual
than that it instantiates the species? We have already noted
Maimonides' reaction to what he took to be Aristotle's
answer (§2.1). Aquinas' distinction proposes an answer to
that question: *esse,* the act of existing determines the individual to be, as its essence determines it to be what it is.

Aquinas adapts an argument from Dionysius (the neo-platonist) to make his point:

> Although living things are more noble than [merely] existing things, nevertheless to-be is nobler than to-live: living things not only have life but have life along with their having being (*De pot.* 7.2.9).

Or, as he will put it elsewhere, the "to-be of living things is to live" (*De anima* 1.14 [209]). If we start, in other words, with living things rather than with the property "life" (or living), then we will be more prone to recognize that their mode of *being* is to live. In returning, then, to speak of this *being,* we will see how inappropriate it was to think of it as a mere presupposition or baseline, to which living was added as a perfection. It is rather that the being of lifeless things is restricted or limited, than that living adds a quality on top of being.

Need the point be *argued* any further? What is required is a shift in our perspectives—one demanded, to be sure, by ambiguities in our language, yet which, once made, sorts them out appropriately. There is in fact a danger in arguing the point further. For our modes of thought are endemically "essentialist," in that we are ever pursuing the question 'what is it?'. The more we speak about *esse,* then, the more prone we will be to turn it into a super-essence.[17] Aquinas would then have led us out of vulgar platonism into neo-platonism! That is why his use of Dionysius was so judicious: it is in regarding living things (through attending to our speech about them) that we realize to-be is nobler than to-live—not by adopting even the vestiges of an emanation scheme.

Allow me to illustrate the point this way. Identifying essence with *esse* in God—the supreme formula for simpleness—would indicate a perfection rather than an impoverishment only if *esse* represented the sum total of perfections. But that would be the case only if there were something beyond essences (and properties) which would actually *be* what those things are determinations of. In short, by predicating *esse* of essence, we would thereby be calling attention to a property which would be received variously by different kinds of being, though totally contained by God. If this were what we were doing, we would be returning full course to what the emanation scheme pictured, and what neoplatonism asserts. Moreover, his argument seemed to presume something like this, when he spoke of "*esse* being determined . . . rather like act by potency," as "in the definition of forms the proper matter appears as a difference: when we say the soul is the act of an organized physical body" (*De pot.* 7.2.9). So as soul is the form of a body, so *esse* will be the form of an essence.

But Aquinas never puts it that way; he offers an analogy of essence to *esse* as matter to form, each displaying something of the yet more basic proportion of potency to act.[18] And to say that *esse* is act, and to suggest thereby that we understand it by analogy with act, warns us away from considering it to be a form or essence. And that, I submit, is the real conversion to which Aquinas is inviting us. For we may well negotiate the move from existence as "something happening to" essence to recognizing it to be a sort of perfection. Attention to individuals can often effect that shift in outlook. But when we go on to attempt to characterize that perfection, how are we not to think of it as a property—as a super-essence (or a *haecceity*)?

Moreover, there is evidence to suppose that Ibn-Sina did just that, as his reflections on existence moved beyond "something happening to" essence, yet did so in a manner strictly parallel to his understanding of essence (§2.3). In his marginal comments on the pseudo-*Theology of Aristotle,* he distinguishes "existence in itself" from contingent as well as from necessary existence, noting that "existence in itself, envisaged in itself, is simply existence."[19] One is immediately reminded of his position on essences, taken "absolutely." Aquinas' way of avoiding such a consideration of *esse* (as well as of "absolute essences") will be to keep returning to existing things. There is then for him no "existence in itself"; only what *has* existence by contrast to what *is* existence—and that contrast formulates "the distinction."

We will avoid thinking of existence as a property, then, only with great difficulty. For what is required is that we leave our accustomed modes of thinking—inherently essentialist—and allow ourselves to be introduced into another order—sketched in §2.1.2. It should not be surprising that reflection on the one from whom all else comes would require such an effort; what must be specified is what it amounts to. One conclusion strikes us immediately. If there is no sense to talk of "existence in itself," since doing so will have the effect of making it a property; and if the best we can do is to use this distinction to formulate "the distinction" of creator from creatures, then simpleness must be discussed in that same context. That is, we should not presume that we know what it is to be metaphysically simple and then to proceed to ask whether such a conception offers a proper description of God. We should rather recognize that the affirmation of simpleness is offered as an attempt to formulate "the distinction." There is, in short, no simpleness but God's simpleness.[20]

3.3.2 ON "FORMAL FEATURES"

The best way I know to put this is to remind ourselves that simpleness is not an attribute of God, properly speaking, so much as a "formal feature" of divinity.[21] That is, we do not include 'simpleness' in that list of terms we wish to attribute to God—classically, 'living', 'wise', 'willing'. It is rather that *simpleness* defines the manner in which such properties might be attributed to God. When we say God is simple, we are speaking not about God directly but about God's ontological constitution; just as when we say that Eloise is composite, we are not predicating anything about her in any of the nine recognizable ways of Aristotle. So it would be putting the cart well before the horse to think of *simpleness* as a constituent property of God whose very "existence is a necessary condition of [God's] existence."[22] "Formal properties" are not so much said of a subject, as they are reflected in a subject's very mode of existing, and govern the way in which anything whatsoever might be said of that subject.

This precision regarding God's simpleness will set the stage for a proper consideration of what are normally proposed as attributes of God (Ch. 4). What is essential to recognize here is that these two sets of adjectives correspond to different ontological levels, and hence require a separate treatment. Moreover, simpleness, and the notions which Aquinas will link with it—limitlessness, unchangeableness, and unity—are all to be understood negatively, whereas he will defend a practice of predicating positive attributes. Considerations of analogy, then, properly enter with such attributes; yet the demand for attention to analogous uses of language will be established as one establishes "the distinction" through these formal features of divinity. For it is they that remind us how God transcends our capacity to know objects, and not just quantitatively—there being a lot about God that we don't know; but they remind us in such a way that we will constantly need to ask ourselves *how* our concepts might be used of divinity—not simply whether or not they apply. These considerations alert us that the only alternative to analogous language *in divinis* is unconsciously to treat God as an object in the world—in short, idolatry. Maimonides' intuitions on this score were utterly accurate, as we shall see (Ch. 4).

3.3   The Argument: Parameters for Considering the Divine Nature

The discrimination of formal features from other attributes is corroborated by the structure of Aquinas'

treatment of these basic questions in the *Summa,* as well as
the arguments he offers for them.[23] (There are also parallels
in Ibn-Sina and in Maimonides, yet here the special status
accorded to "essential attributes" seems rather to reflect a
concern for those which would characterize divinity *as
such,* by contrast with relational terms following upon
creation.[24]) The arguments are illustrative in that none of
them pretends to know what it might *mean* to deny, say,
composition, or limits, or change, but each proceeds to the
denial because it can do no other. The negative character
of the formal features, in other words, is *displayed* in the
forced negations of the argument.

So God lacks the composition of body and soul (1.3.1)
and of matter and form (1.3.2), because pure act admits of
no potentiality; of essence and supposition because of
lacking matter (1.3.3), of essence and *esse* because no prior
cause could bring God into being (1.3.4); of genus and
species because nothing specifies *being* nor is being a genus
(1.3.5), of substance and accident because nothing need be
added to nor can be said to "happen to" God (1.3.6).
Aquinas' conclusion is that God is utterly simple, for there
is no way that any of the modes of logical or ontological
composition make sense in treating divinity (1.3.7). Yet
even here, he warns us away from conceiving God's simpleness on the model most congenial to us—form—by insisting
that such a One cannot be thought of as the form of the
world, but must subsist. It is "the distinction" which
simpleness must secure. If the world can be presented as
God's body, creation remains an empty phrase.[25]

God cannot be said to be in a genus, then, even "the
first in the genus of substance, but is 'first' outside of any
genus with respect to the whole of being (*esse*)" (1.3.6.2).
This disclaimer is reminiscent of Avicenna's unwillingness
to countenance quiddity of divinity, and also shows
Aquinas' desire to escape the implications of 'first' in an
emanation scheme. Taken together with the warning not
to construe simpleness on the model of form, it makes a

strong plea to raise one's intellectual vision beyond essences to "pure act." The culminating statement of simpleness is clearly the identification of essence with existence, where "*esse* is to be compared to essence as act to potency," so that one must say that "in divinity essence cannot be different from God's own to-be" (1.3.4). This identification forbids us from considering God's essence in the line of properties, and invites us to recognize the limits of our conceptual powers. The affirmation of God's simpleness, then, is not an ordinary statement about God, so much as an assertion showing where "the distinction" is to be drawn, and in what directions we should look to overcome our endemic "essentialism." Only then will we recognize it to be a perfection in God.[26]

The further "formal features" of limitlessness, unchangeableness, and oneness follow directly from the identification of essence with *esse* in God, together with the stipulation that *esse* is ever comparable to essences as act to potency.[27] For, as we have seen, what then determines *esse* will be essence, not as form determines matter, but rather as act is limited by potency. The essence that is simply to-be, then, can in no way limit its *esse*. Moreover, it is this feature which also connects the creator with all of creation: "since the essence of God is *esse* itself, it is proper that created *esse* be the effect proper to God"; but *esse* is that which is most inward to each thing and most profoundly within all things . . . so God may be said to be in all things, and intimately so" (1.8.1). Where the emanation scheme supplied a formal and imaginative connection, Aquinas reaches for an even more intimate linkage by making a move beyond formal structures to the very to-be of things.

Similarly, what is simply to-be is not in a process of becoming, so not subject to change. God's "capacity" to act is hardly in question; it is simply that divine action does not involve movement from potency to act, so is only metaphorically a capacity. And what is not subject to change is not itself in time, so God must be eternal. Not, once more, that we have a notion of eternity which we are asserting of God, but that one of the formal features following from the identification of essence with *esse* in God (which best expresses divine simpleness) is God's eternity.[28] For, as Aquinas puts it, "eternity is the measure of *esse* . . . as time is the measure of motion" (1.10.4). So given the fact that God is God's own to-be, "God is not only eternal but [God's] own eternity (*sua aeternitas*)" (1.10.2). Like simpleness and limitlessness and unchangeableness before it, eternity makes no sense unless it be God's eternity. The only means we have of gaining access to these formal features is through the ladder Aquinas provides: "*esse* as the actuality of all things and of all forms" (1.4.1.3).

The final formal feature, culminating Aquinas' treatment, is God's oneness. So it must be intended to meet the concerns of Jewish and of Muslim thinkers that God's unity be the resplendent feature. Aquinas reiterates Maimonides' complaint that it would be "absurd to ascribe to Him—whose existence is necessary, who is truly simple, to whom composition cannot attach in any way—the accident of oneness . . .; oneness is not a notion that is superadded to His essence" (*Guide* 1.57). In fact, the "one that is convertible with being [cannot] add anything beyond the substance of a thing"—as Avicenna thought—under pain of infinite regress (*ST* 1.11.1.1). So, Aquinas avers, we must rather be speaking of a "oneness signifying nothing other than undivided being" (1.11.1). And that we can certainly deliver in a God conceived as utterly simple. If the other formal features were at the service of "the distinction," this summary one seems more directly concerned with returning the philosophical treatment to its religious roots, showing how profoundly it concurs with the act of faith common to Jew, Christian, and Muslim:

> Hear, O Israel, God your God is one . . .
> We believe in One God . . .
> There is no god but Allah . . .

4. Names of God:
Attributes of Divine Nature

IF KNOWING WHO GOD is entails knowing what God is, we must also recognize that knowing what God is involves knowing what can properly be said of God. If the preceding chapter was more expressly metaphysical this one will deal more with linguistic matters, but the two are connected. Moreover, if the upshot of being simple is that God is unknowable, then what of all those things we do say about God? Are the philosophers too austere? For we find ourselves speaking about God, and even more relevantly, revelation introduces us to God in human speech. So if philosophical theologians have to say that God is utterly simple, believers have to say that God is just, faithful, compassionate, and the like.

How can we relate these two concerns? And how do the things we say of God relate to our wider discourse? These two questions will structure this chapter: (A) relating philosophical constraints with religious concerns, (B) relating those concerns with wider human culture. In the Islamic development, the debate was clear-cut: one either sided with the philosophers, securing divine transcendence through asserting simpleness, or one insisted that the "ninety-nine beautiful names of God" nullified such a position from the side of the Qur'an.

Seemingly unable to reconcile opposition between simpleness and multiplicity of attributes, the orthodox position contented itself with asserting the transcendence of the God named in ninety-nine different ways. Since this strategy rendered the philosophical position heterodox, some sought ways of mitigating the differences—notably Abu Hashim.[1] But the lines had been drawn, and philosophy itself helped to consolidate the stand-off by construing these attributes as ordinary adjectives modifying a subject. Moreover, Islam's predilection for clear speech led few to question this position. The revelation of the Qur'an had no difficulty making its meaning felt, thanks to the exquisite Arabic of the book. So whatever would be said there—of God or any other thing—would surely refer unequivocally to its subject.

Maimonides was explicitly concerned to relate the meaning of scriptural terms to a wider cultural context. Yet he found it impossible to reconcile the sense which the Torah conveyed ("using the language of men") with that required to speak properly of God. As a result, he had to insist that we were always speaking improperly, if we thought that we knew what we were saying, in calling God *just*. When some Muslim thinkers did venture a reason why certain terms might be used of God as well as of creatures, they were prone to note a difference of modality: what is contingent with us is necessary to God; what we exhibit in time characterizes God externally. Maimonides had no patience with *modes*: "there cannot be any belief in the unity of God except by admitting that He is one simple substance, without any composition or plurality of elements" (1.51). That confession forbids us to think of God as "having attributes," and sound philosophy permits no middle ground as though "the attributes of God are neither His essence nor anything extraneous to His essence" (1.51). *Modes* offers no more than verbal relief. To one inquiring, then, how God might know or be just, he could only respond: *not* in our way.

Maimonides was correct, of course, to reject something between an attribute and an utterly simple nature—something which its proponents called a "mode." For such a middle position finds no reflection in our use of language, and so will be intrinsically unstable. Yet there is a more natural use of 'mode', which Aquinas adapted to this context, corresponding to our *manner* of asserting something to be the case *in divinis*. Such an approach, however, asks to attend more closely to the ways in which certain terms can be—and sometimes must be—employed beyond their normal range. Yet Maimonides was disinclined to exercise expressions in such a way; he seemed to prefer contrasting a determinate philosophical sense with the frankly anthropomorphic uses of the Torah (1.53). This predilection deprived him of the middle ground Aquinas would occupy by distinguishing terms with genuinely analogical uses from those which could only be employed metaphorically.

Put simply: Maimonides was unable formally to distinguish God's wisdom from God's face. As a result, I shall argue, he could only *assert* that God was wise, but not "by wisdom" and hence in no way *like* our manner of being wise (1.57, 1.53). Aquinas will agree with that basic contention, yet move one step beyond bald assertion, by noting that terms like 'just' can (and must) be employed analogously if they are to do the jobs we want them to do. As a result, they are not only susceptible of a vast differentiation in meaning, but also in *mode* of predication.[2]

The fact that 'just' in its normal use is never a merely descriptive predicate, then, suggests a more positive way of rendering Maimonides' insistence that God is wise, but not "by wisdom." That is, God's *manner* of being wise is such that being God is to be the very norm and source of wisdom. (That contention captures the scriptures' insistence, embodied in the drama of Job and formulated by Isaiah: "My thoughts are not your thoughts, my ways not your ways—it is the lord who speaks" (55.8)—a favorite verse of Maimonides.) Understood in this way, one is more inclined to accept God's manner of being wise as different from the way anything else could be wise. And if we were to show that God is not the sort of being who *has* attributes, then a path might be opened to asserting wisdom of God in a manner quite different from asserting anything else to be wise, yet respectful of the senses the term 'wise' can sustain, and coherent as an assertion about divinity. In short, the mode of being we attribute to divinity will govern *how* we might attribute those features necessary to being divine. Abu Hashim's intuition about "modes" may prove more suggestive than Maimonides, following Ibn-Sina and al-Ghazali, could have suspected.

4.1   Towards the Mode of Being Proper to Attributes in God

How then might we characterize the mode of being proper to attributes *in divinis*? As has been intimated, this will not prove an easy task. In fact, if one begins with attributes, asking how *they* might inhere in God, the *prima facie* conflict with divine simplicity faces us with a celebrated impasse.[3] That impasse became the scene of bitter collisions opposing philosophically-minded Muslims to the vast majority who took their cues from the Qur'an. The devotion of believers spontaneously attached to the evocative names of God, and when these beliefs met the philosophers' insistence on simpleness, the philosophical doctrine could hardly stand the onslaught. Those insisting on the *reality* of divine attributes won the day, even if they could only assert that such manifest multiplicity need not compromise their fundamental belief in the unity of God—the celebrated *tawhid*.

Maimonides' expressed clarifications—"God lives, but not *by* life"—show how clear he was about subordinating attributes to God's unitary nature, yet his celebrated agnosticism regarding them brought him also into conflict with the religious-minded in his community. My contention is that he had recourse to so extreme a solution because he began with attributes—taken as properties—and could find no coherent way to *attribute* them to the one God.[4] How could the God who revealed itself to be one *have* such a bevy of attributes? *We* must attribute all such perfections to God, of course, but how God possesses them, and hence what they amount to in divinity, must escape us entirely. Such agnosticism offered him a dignified way to continue to affirm God's transcendent unity while praying the psalms, yet more flexible philosophical strategies could have opened alternative paths.

We can begin to develop those by reflecting on attributes of things which have determinate natures. We can expect Thomas to know, since knowing is proper to humans. We can attribute knowledge to individuals because it is a property of human nature. Moreover, when the capacity to know follows from the nature, we are dealing with a property in the strict sense (by contrast with an accident.) To be able to know, then, is a necessary condition for being human, although it cannot be identified with the nature since it is a specific capacity. For the most part, a definite nature brings many specific capacities with it, and we know what that nature is when we can show how such capacities are *proper* to it. That is the scheme which Aristotle left us.

The scheme presumes, moreover, that each nature is in potency to its proper fulfillment, so it employs these powers to carry out its proper function to "do its thing." What we call properties, I am suggesting, presume this situation in which they function as *powers*. (In an explicitly Jewish, Christian, or Muslim perspective, the situation is one of created natures.) What if the nature were perfectly actualized? In an idealized artificial model, a perfectly running machine would simply be what it does. If we were to project a perfectly integrated human being, we could speak (as Augustine would) of the different levels ordered to a transcendent and transforming goal, and hence aligned and attuned with one another; or we could put it as a Zen master might: "what I do is me." For in act, I *am* knower, seeker, lover; it is not the power that knows, but *I* who know—by my intellect.[5]

Since, of course, I am not always knowing, nor is the machine always running, we must speak of persons or machines as *having* certain capacities. But if we were able to speak of something whose nature was simply to-be, and hence was ever in act, these reflections could help us see how and why we would be inclined to identify such a being's attributes with its essence. For they would not then be powers which this being needed to realize its [divine] nature, and certainly not accidents which happen to accrue to this individual. Rather, it would simply be the case that to be God is to be wise, as it is the case that to be God is to-be. For since being such a one entails being ever in act, it would know, not by a part of itself, but by its whole self. Not that we can clearly know what we intend to say by that assertion; it is rather that we have no warrant for asserting otherwise, since what is in act has no *powers* by which it acts.

The two-fold realization demanded here offers a way through Maimonides' dilemma by giving systematic form to his insights: since we must affirm God to be "absolutely one" (1.52) and that "his essence includes all His perfections" (1.59), there cannot be "in God something additional to His essence, in the same way as attributes are joined our essence" (1.56). So we must say that God "knows, without possessing the attribute of knowledge" (1.57). And if our language can only attribute such perfections by relying on the metaphysical scheme whereby properties are something "superadded to this essence" (1.59), then to "believe in the reality of the attributes [is] to say that God is one subject of which several things are predicated" (1.60). In short, "these who admit the attributes of God do not consider them as identical with His essence, but as extraneous elements" (1.60).

But what if one were able to detach the metaphysical scheme from this admittedly unique act of prediction— something Maimonides approaches in his sketch of the activity of praising God (1.59)? To do so, we would have to keep two "formal facts" in mind at once: (1) that our habitual manner of attributing characteristics presupposes the dispositional structure proper to created natures sketched out above; and (2) that an uncaused being in which "existence and essence are perfectly identical" (1.57) would be entirely in act, by which act it would live, know, and will. So the insistence that God's attributes be "identical with [God's] essence" (1.60) cannot be a straightforward claim that certain properties be identical with the divine essence, but must contain an implicit plea to alter our understanding of the relation of attribute to essence in divinity. And the activity of altering that understanding will lead us to one more way of uniquely characterizing what remains properly indefinable—or knowing what is unknowable.

4.2   The Potentialities of Language

Because Maimonides could not see how we could alter our characteristic manner of attributing when it came to divinity, nor could he attenuate the traditional confession that God is one, he had recourse to a radical agnosticism regarding the statements we use to praise God: "there is, in no way or sense, anything common to the attributes predicated of God, and those used in reference to ourselves; they have only the same names, and nothing else is common to them" (1.56). This was the only strategy open to him because his analysis of *similarity* turned on "the same definition [applying] to both [uses of an expression]" (1.56). Aquinas proved able to speak more positively of divine attributes because he did not so much ask for the meaning as look to the uses of a set of privileged expressions.

So it appears that one will better be able to hold the two formal facts just mentioned in tension, the more one attends to language use. To recognize how our notions of attribute (or property) are imbedded in an habitual use of language is to leave the way open to conceiving another manner of predication when confronted with a radically different sort of being: the uncaused One whose essence is to be. And the way would be negotiable—rather than merely proposed—were there certain expressions susceptible of shifting both meaning and mode when predicated. Perfection-terms turn out to be just such a set, as Aquinas displays the features attendant on their use, in a treatment which could be taken as an extended commentary on Maimonides' insistence that God's "essence include all His perfections" (1.59).[6]

We will better be able to appreciate the moves Aquinas makes in his question devoted to the "Names of God" (1.13), however, if we place it in the context of his extended development of God's simpleness and oneness (1.3-11). For these "formal features" of divinity, on his account, are shown to entail goodness, limitlessness (infinity) and unchangeableness, and these taken together will determine how it is that the more characteristic perfections must be said of God. *Goodness,* here taken as a formal feature of divinity, will explicitly license the predication of perfection-terms, and the other dimensions of simpleness—limitlessness and unchangeableness—will determine *how* they can be said of God. The semantic features proper to perfection-terms make them susceptible of such a use, but the defining characteristics of the "first being" as the One whose essence is to-be, make this unusual mode of predication imperative.[7]

Rather than beginning with many properties and going on to ask how they might be predicated of the divine nature, Aquinas begins with an account of that nature in its required simpleness, to show that its being and its activity will have to be the originating source of specific perfections as well. Approaching the question from this direction allows him to show how what is "absolutely One" (*Guide* 1.52) may and must be understood to be many without derogating from oneness. But how can the *direction* of an exposition make so telling a difference? It seems as neat a trick to show how one can be many as to identify many with the one.

4.2.1 AQUINAS: FORMAL FEATURES

Let us look at the way Aquinas argues for God's being identified with divine goodness, the divine act of understanding, and divine willing, to see whether his actual procedure offers any clues to the puzzle. Each argument turns on the crucial formula for simpleness: God lacks even that composition remaining to the most spiritual of created beings. For if such beings have no intrinsic reason not to be, neither do they have a *reason* to be. For nothing is its own *raison d'etre*, Aquinas insists, except the one from whom everything else orginates. And the neat way of stating that is to show that God's nature is simply to-be, or as Maimonides put it: "God alone is that being [whose] existence and essence are perfectly identical" (1.57). For Aquinas, too, this inevitable conclusion offers the best way of expressing simpleness, and from such ontological simpleness are derived the consequent formal features, as well as every essential attribute.[8]

The source of that derivation lies in the basic analogy Aquinas adopts for the feature which Maimonides (and Ibn-Sina before him) had identified as *existence*. For Aquinas, this is always "being in act" (*ens actu*), "the act of being" (*actus essendi*), or simply "to-be" (*esse*) where the infinitive form connotes an activity.[9] Thus existence, for Aquinas, intends to assert far more than "the fact that a state of affairs obtains (or *is exemplified*)," precisely by supplanting the neutral 'obtains' or the evasive 'is exemplified' by the analogy of *action*. By eschewing the noun 'existence' (*existentia*) and employing the infinitive 'to-be' (*esse*) or the more explicit 'act of being' (*actus essendi*), Aquinas wants to underscore that 'to-be' is itself a perfection-expression. So deliberate a choice of language intends to emphasize at once Aristotle's predilection for existing things as the paradigm instances of *substance,* and the provenance of all existing things from a creative source whose "proper effect is the to-be of things" (1.8.1).

God is identified with divine goodness, then, because what accounts for the perfection proper to each thing stems from its being in act (*esse actu in unoquoque est bonum ipsius*).[10] Created things have need of powers to attain a goal extrinsic to themselves, but since God alone is being in act—indeed its own to-be (*ipsum suum esse*)—God must also be its own goodness. Since what essentially exists (*per essentiam*) has no potential to realize, there can be no gap between its being and its perfection, as there must be in what participates in the being of that essentially existing one (*ens per participationem*).[11] So what must be represented as something additional to a created nature—achievement of its potential—must by the same token be ingredient in the uncreated One and identified with the divine nature, since God has no potential to realize but is essentially in act.

The same logic governs what we must assert regarding the divine act of understanding and of willing. For the act of understanding is to the intellect as *esse* to essence. But if the divine essence is to-be (*esse*), then the divine intellect is the divine act of understanding. And divine intellect cannot be other than the divine essence—indeed, need not be, as we have seen, since divine activity needs no additional powers—so God's act of understanding must be identified with the divine essence (*CG* 1.45, *ST* 1.14.4). Here Aquinas adapts Alfarabi's identification of ["power of"] understanding, act of understanding, and thing understood in the "first being," to show how identifying the divine act of understanding with its to-be demands that "this act of understanding be simple, eternal and unvarying, and ever in act, thereby displaying (*probata sunt*) everything claimed for the divine to-be" (*CG* 1.45). Moreover, since willing follows directly upon understanding for Aquinas, with the single difference that its action terminates in the action executed, "divine willing too must be [contained in] God's to-be."[12]

Note how each of these arguments turns on the identity of essence with *esse* in divinity, and they cumulatively underscore the uncomparable *unity* of God—the keystone of Maimonides' systematic treatment, and the centerpiece of Islamic theology: *tawhid*. They could not even pretend to be arguments, however, if we consider *esse* as one property among others, or if we were to presume the attributes essential to divinity to be "objects distinct from him, uncreated by him, and [to] exist necessarily."[13]

For on such an ontology, it would remain problematic how all these things come to be joined in God, and yet more puzzling why they should be said to be identified with divine nature. If, on the other hand, "existence" does not name a property of things, but rather refers to that *to-be* which was presupposed by Aristotle and considered by Jew and Muslim alike as the creative emanation from and effect of a creator, then the arguments proceed. For if God, as the originating source of all, must be God's own to-be, then all perfections will be "contained in" divinity. That must be said, because *esse* is not just the presupposition but the source of all achievements; and the one that is its own to-be will have no need of being perfected and hence have no goal outside itself.

4.2.2 MAIMONIDES: UNITY AMONG MANY NAMES

There is nothing associated with divinity as Islamic philosophers will put it, for God has no need of another (or of the world) to be God.[14] Aquinas expresses it by saying that God is *sua bonitas*, God's own goodness: the key to identifying the attributes which are perfection-terms with the divine essence. For the ways in which the psalmist extolls the God of Israel amount to a catalogue of aspirations, yet since "God is not ordered to anything extraneous as an end but is rather the ultimate end of all things" (*ST* 1.6.3), the only way such aspirations can be *attributed to* God will be to identify them with God's very being. That same argument regarding God's perfection led Maimonides to insist that we cannot attribute anything to God, as we have noted. So his task would be to show how so manifestly "unbiblical" a teaching offers "appropriate expression to the biblical principle [that God is a] hidden God who created the world out of nothing, not in order to increase the good . . . but . . . in absolute freedom."[15] Underscoring God's hiddenness, the "names of God" become icons or images, with the most sacred name—the one given from God to us—quite securely mysterious since we understand it not at all, "knowing so little of Hebrew!"[16]

Yet what controls the biblical use of names, and allows us to discriminate among the images, will be God's unity, which Maimonides secures by adopting Alfarabi's identification of intellect, act of understanding, and things understood, in divinity (1.68). This final speculation on divine unity can be considered to be Maimonides' reaching for a *formulation* of unity which will allow him to establish "formal features" of divinity in the face of explicitly achieving "positive attributes." Not that he made such a distinction, either in the structure of his treatment or in so many words, but it is possible so to understand him. And helpful as well, for if God's perfection offers the key in Aquinas' case to identifying attributes with the divine essence, and in Maimonides' case to denying positive attribution to divinity, then they must have different ways of handling attribution, and may even be employing different models for perfection. (As we shall see, it will be a little bit of both).

The utter simplicity of God dominates Maimonides'

treatment, so that divinity cannot be in need of additional powers to do what it does. Put philosophically, all God's perfections must exist in actuality; nothing may belong to God which exists potentially in any way whatsoever (1.52, 1.53). In this respect, then, while we speak of God as existing, living, powerful, or knowing, such language must not imply a likeness between these attributes essential to God and those said of us, as though God possessed them to a superlative degree (1.56). As Maimonides is careful to put it, "God exists, but not through an existence other than His essence" (1.57), and the same conditions hold for asserting that God lives, is powerful, or knows.

What is clearly at stake here is articulating a mode of being proper to the source of all, and securing the first being's "distinction" from all that is. Once having accomplished that, it will be exceedingly odd to *attribute* something to such a One. This reading of Maimonides is supported by his reasons for preferring negative attributes, since these are more apt to be "used in order to conduct the mind towards that which must be believed with respect to Him, for no notion of multiplicity can attach to Him in any respect on account of them" (1.58). Maimonides goes on to sketch out a dialectic of "negative knowing," showing how we might exploit the *difference* to learn how to appreciate what looks to be a lack as a perfection in divinity (1.59). The alternative, he fears, can only be idolatry: worshipping a false (non-existent) God tailored to our own image (1.60). The Torah, however, demands rigorous philosophical abnegation, as his summary statement shows: "there is accordingly an existent whom none of the existent things He has brought into existence resembles, and who has nothing in common with them in any respect" (1.58).

If we underscore "in any *respect*," Aquinas will agree, for perfection terms can be used in a way which outstrips determinate *respects,* and *existing* is not a feature of whatever exists. So Maimonides and Aquinas do not differ so much in their formal requirements for divinity, as in their grasp of the semantics of the terms we can attribute to God, and hence their accounts of what attribution *in divinis* amounts to. Each is intent on securing a coherent philosophical articulation of "the distinction" of God from the world. And Maimonides gives direct expression to God's uniqueness by adopting Alfarabi's identification of intellect, act of understanding, and things understood, to characterize the divine essence (1.68).

In effect, then, Maimonides takes an activity—understanding—and does with it what Aquinas does with *esse*: by identifying the divine essence with all activity, each wishes to show the uniqueness of divinity by displaying its "distinction" from all else that exists. They both invite philosophical thinkers to reach towards a yet higher perspective: Maimonides, by proposing that we attempt to conceive such an act of understanding; Aquinas, that we begin to think of existing as an act. Aquinas' strategy is more comprehensive and coherent, since that *act* can logically "contain" all perfections; whereas Maimonides' divine act of understanding not only contradicts his stricture of absolute homonymy regarding language about divinity but demands that he reduce all the other attributes to this one (cf. 1.53, where "life" is construed as "knowledge").[17]

And he must do this because Alfarabi's formula functions for him as an articulation of divine unity, and hence as establishing the "formal features" for predicting anything of God. Moreover, that formula was licensed by what Maimonides had identified as the image (*zelem*) of God in man: "on account of the Divine intellect with which man has been endowed, he is said to have been made in the form of likeness of the Almighty" (1.1). This reading of the Genesis account of creation locates the divine image in "the intellect [by which] man distinguishes between the true and the false" (1.2)—the speculative, not the practical, intellect. On the strength of this perfection God was able to interact with us: "on account of this gift of intellect man was addressed by God, and received His commandments" (1.2); yet when Adam disobeyed, giving "way to desires which had their source in his imagination and to the gratification of his bodily appetites, . . . he was punished by the loss of part of that intellectual faculty which he had previously possessed" (1.2). Henceforth, we had to become preoccupied with 'right' and 'wrong'—"terms employed in the science of apparent truths (morals)"—and "wholly absorbed in the study of what is proper and what improper" (1.2), as opposed to what is true or false.

So our inability to speak truthfully of God is explained philosophically by the impropriety of predicating anything at all *of* divinity; and theologically, by our loss of the fullness of the divine image in our mind. Not even the Torah can correct the disorientation which results, for it must cater to our preoccupation with "a knowledge of apparent truths . . .: what is proper and what improper" (1.2). The best we can hope is that right practice will direct us towards the "necessary truths" we cannot know. And our fate becomes much worse for Maimonides, as he identifies speculative knowledge as the perfection proper to man. And a speculative knowing, moreover, which he characterizes as an "intellectual perception" (1.4) of "the true form of an object" (1.3). Such an outlook would not be congenial to Aquinas' proposals of a progressive, analogical grasp of something which our conceptions can at best "imperfectly signify."[18] So Maimonides' model for human perfection, together with his patterns of predication, directed him to an account of attributing perfections to God different from that which Aquinas was able to fashion. The purpose of this comparison has been to focus that difference, as well as to underscore their common intent: to assure the uniqueness of a God "distinct from" the world.

4.3   *Formal Statements and Divinity*

What of those statements which are true as part of logical or mathematical systems—which do not need to be judged to be true, except in the remote sense that one accepts the logic or mathematics in question? As truths of logic, are they not anterior to creation? Moreover, if "abstract objects are also naturally thought of as *necessary* features of reality, as objects whose non-existence is impossible," how can such a realm be said to depend upon God for its existence?[19] And how can God's nature be conceived in relation to them?

The question itself is partly a function of ontological perspectives. An Aristotelian is more prone to begin with substances as what primarily exist, asking in turn what can be said *of* them. To such a one, accidental predication remains secondary to essential predication, so that properties will always be considered in relation to an essence, whose status as a predicate remains privileged throughout all considerations, since it renders the formula for substance itself. A more Platonist ontology, on the other hand, tends to regard all predicates as naming things, and consider essences, along with the other things named, to be properties.[20] Without assigning a priority to essence as the formula for substance, properties will "naturally" be regarded as prior to the thing of which they are predicated, and puzzles like the following will be generated:

> Suppose God has essentially the property of being omnipotent and suppose that property is an object distinct from him, is uncreated by him and exists necessarily. Then in some sense he does depend on that property.[21]

We have seen how Ibn-Sina tended to split the difference on these two perspectives, by focusing more on essence than on its connection with primary substance, and in being led to speak of existence as "coming to" essence, so that one might regard it as an accident. So the pull to property-language is a strong one, even if one might *not* quite regard it as 'natural' to think of the world and things as composed of "abstract objects . . . whose non-existence is impossible." One might consider it far more natural to keep existing things clearly in focus as the items of the world, and find Aquinas' analogy of existence (*esse*) to act a particularly felicitous way of underscoring their primacy —in short, of confirming an Aristotelian perspective by enhancing it.

Yet the question remains, even if the terms are less problematic for someone like Aquinas: what about "necessary truths"? How are they related to divinity? The shape of Aquinas' own response is well known. Following Augustine, these become the "divine ideas"—not, however, that *by which* God understands, but that *which* God understands (*ST* 1.15, *CG* 2.51-54). That is, Aquinas insists that God's knowing is not propositional, and that God's creative activity should not be considered literally after the fashion of a craftsman who must look to blueprints, or be thought to work *from* an idea. If that be the case, however, they would seem to idle "in the mind of God," if not clutter that utterly simple act of understanding.

Aquinas' description of their role is illuminating:

> God, in knowing his essence as imitable in this particular way by this particular creature, knows his essence as the nature and idea proper to that creature (*ST* 1.15.2).

It is as though God, in creating, understands that for a created nature to imitate the divine nature, it will have to be so structured. The "ideas" which convey that structure to us can be likened (in God) to the "form in the mind of the builder" (1.15.2), without thereby asserting that God creates *by them* as a builder does. Similarly, such a conception of their role finesses the question: does God create them too? For they rather express the structure creation will assume *as* God's creation—"imitating the divine essence."

In that respect, then, the *ideas* are dependent upon God's nature, though not on God's will. What is said to be "in the mind of God" in an exemplary way is what God understands must be the case *if* the divine essence is to be initiated by such a nature. They would seem, then, to function more like rules of inference, or like the constraints of matter, purpose, and agents in building something, than like constituent parts of the created things. Here is where the Platonist picture of a plethora of properties finds itself at odds with Aquinas' more Aristotelian scheme of the various ways in which substances can be said to be. That the world is so structured becomes the working presupposition of scientific inquiry; that anything we could properly call a "world" would have to be structured in some fashion gives that inquiry its intellectual edge. Yet structural (or formal) features differ from other constituents in that things are not made *of* them.

Another way of articulating this role for truths of logic and mathematics is to recall that the ruling notion for God's creative knowing (in Aquinas) is practical knowledge, as the controlling image is that of a maker (*ST* 1.14.8). By insisting that the "divine ideas" be instrumental to God's making, he is underscoring once more "the distinction," showing God to be utterly first, creating by giving *esse* and intending the "good order of the universe," in such a way that all emanates from God. In his extended treatment in *de Veritate,* he asks whether "divine ideas pertain to speculative knowing or only to practical" (3.3). As ideas, they must belong to both, but in God "*idea* properly speaking regards practical knowledge."

In sum, what we discover to be truths of logic or mathematics become instrumental to creation as the necessary condition of the divine nature being imitated in such a way.

So identifying their role allows them to share the hypo-
thetical necessity proper to contingent being: if there is to
be such a creation, it must issue in such a manner. If this is
what Aquinas makes of locating "necessary truths" as
"ideas in the mind of God," it seems to be a quite natural
conceptual move, although a number of questions remain
about their relation to the one divine essence.[22]

As *ideas,* they will be timeless, hence it makes no sense
to ask when they *began* to exist in the mind of God, nor
would it make sense to ask directly whether they are
created or uncreated, since they are rather conditions attendant upon God's creating. They would then share the status
of God's creative intent, co-eternal with God yet realized
in time, and so dependent upon that creative intent. This is
simply what it is to be a formal, timeless truth, with no
implications whatsoever regarding their having "always
existed and . . . never *begun* to exist."[23] Unless, of course,
'existing' approaches a merely honorific status. For Aquinas,
God alone is eternal, not timeless; while God's creative
knowing will express itself in *ways* which also admit of a
formal consideration to which time is irrelevant.[24] Hence
they can be said to be "timeless truths."

Such a scenario, however, is itself beholden to "the distinction" of God from the world, wherein God's uniqueness
is expressed by the identity of *esse* with essence in divinity.
If this also be taken as expressing what we mean by God's
being necessary—a term more congenial to Ibn-Sina than to
Aquinas—that necessity will not consist in God's existing
in all possible worlds, nor need God's free and creative
activity be pictured as "deciding" which of such "worlds"
to "actualize."[25] For the uniqueness and necessity secured
by identifying essence with *esse* in divinity is logically
prior to any worlds at all, and the activity of creating will
bespeak a divine freedom, which deals not in choices but
in *present* responsiveness. However descriptions of the relations of eternity to time may inevitably escape us, the

order of *presence to* must be respected. To say that what we know as "timeless truths" are "in the mind of" an eternal creator as that which is attendant upon such one's freely creating, yet not that *by which* divinity knows itself to be inevitable by its creation, is to make such *ideas* clear instruments of the divine activity of creating, and so issue a final statement of "the distinction" of God from the world.

5. God's Knowledge of Particulars

WITH SUCH AN ACCOUNT of divinity: one whose very essence is to-be, such that the formal features of simpleness, perfection, unchangeableness, limitlessness and oneness will attend the articulation of that divine nature as well as structure anything said of it—how can we hope to relate God to God's world? If the interests of distinguishing creator from creation be served by such a transcendental grammar, what steps need to be taken to articulate the positive side of the creator-creation relationship? It is well known that many today would prefer to elide the distinction so as to be able to conceptualize the relation more "adequately," that is, in terms more comprehensible to accepted philosophical parlance. Their motivation—in part religious, in part philosophical, is reinforced by a reading of the "classical doctrine" which links it to Hellenic archetypal preferences for permanence over change, impassivity over suffering, and the like. Part of my motivation in this exercise of comparative reading has been to recover an historical situation quite detached from such archetypal constraints, to discover how concerned they were to find an "adequate conceptuality" for the faith—and in fact for three distinct faiths.

It should be clear by now that Ibn-Sina's division of being into necessary and possible beings was less a fascination with modalities than it was a way of using such modalities to characterize the One whose essence is existence (8.4, 346:12). Similarly, Maimonides brings Arab philosophy together with the name God gave to Moses, to yield "the necessarily existent" (1.63 [Pines]). These attempts precisely to recast a philosophical tradition so as to articulate the One proclaimed to be beyond conventional formulation form the living context for Aquinas' elucidation as that One to be whom is simply to-be (1.3.4). And that final formulation would render a general characterization of God's "powers"—notably knowing and will—unproblematic in the face of the overriding constraint of simpleness, for the One whose nature is to-be cannot but possess all the perfections of being (1.4.1).

5.1   Conceiving God's Relation to World

Maimonides had stated as much (1.55), but his grasp of the semantic structure of attribution, together with an unwillingness to countenance analogical similarities, forced him to eschew positively ascribing knowledge to the One. Gersonides was later to take him to task for explicitly denying what his entire treatment of divinity had to presume and what he had explicitly stated—"that all perfections must really exist in God."[1] But that part of the story need not concern us here; what is unquestionable here is that the only way for such a One to relate to the world will be by way of knowing and loving. The only way of relating to another intrinsically without requiring a common measure or reciprocity is the intentional one of knowing and loving. So one can be related to another in sharing a common species, or in being actively engaged in a shared enterprise, or extrinsically in a limitless variety of respects, but the only way open for the One to relate to everything else existing in virtue of it, is through knowing and loving.

So those are the terms in which this chapter will pursue God's knowledge, notably of individuals. Not as a detached discussion of divine epistemology, as it were; but as the necessary complement to the preceding two chapters: how relate such a God to the world. So the sense in which my last generalization is not quite true—there are other ways of relating One to many, emanation being a favorite, especially of the Arabs—will also contribute to the overall goal of this exposition. For we shall see how Ibn-Sina's treatment of God's knowledge of particulars was hampered exactly to the extent that he relied upon an emanation scheme to relate necessary to possible being. Where an inevitable (and hence not yet fully intentional) emanation serves as the vehicle of knowing, the limits of one's knowing must conform to the contours of the scheme.[2] So a causal scheme relating the first being to everything else will have to be transformed into a thoroughly intentional mode of causality, lest the first being become bound up with world-process, or restricted to knowing the general principles governing that process.

Aristotle had supplied the tools for articulating such an intentional causality in his notion of practical knowledge: both doing and making. Since his first mover, however, was not a creator, that one's knowing was of a speculative form, focused on itself. Without losing sight of that dimension of self-knowledge, Jewish, Muslim and Christian thinkers would add a practical component when it came to characterizing the One as creator. And with that practical knowing would naturally come an inclination towards what was done or made as "God saw that it was good": the natural complement to knowing is loving. In the subsequent development of Aristotle, however, the crucial issue became: which mode predominated—speculative or practical? The difference between speculative and practical knowing turns out to be a useful way of distinguishing neoplatonic emanation schemes from a conceptuality more proper to creation—a task not always easy to do. For the Muslim philosophers' predilection for emanation reflected their conviction that divine immutability and simplicity could only be safeguarded by the eternal and necessary emanation of the world.[3] As Muslims, they then had to assimilate that process to creation. Yet the religious thinkers sensed a gap between such a theory and the Qur'an's insistence that "your lord is the creator who is truly creator, the one who knows all things" (15:86).

One way of marking the difference is to oppose the philosopher's intellectual scheme with God's sovereign will. And that was a typical reaction of Muslim religious thinkers, as it would later be of fourteenth-century Western Christians.[4] The way to a middle ground, however, lies in grasping the sense of the emanation scheme. Based on Aristotle's sketch of a cosmology of spheres, the scheme elaborated by Alfarabi and incorporated virtually intact by Ibn-Sina, soon detached itself from celestial matters. It became a mirror of the Neoplatonic ascent to the One, a perfect unrolling of the pattern of intellectual ascent so that the structure of reality might embody intellect, macrocosm reflecting the microcosm. Not unlike the way in which Aristotle often inverts the maxim "art imitates nature" to illustrate the structure of natural things from artifacts, Avicenna's fascination with cosmic emanation bespeaks his "quest for an intellectual gnosis."[5]

So God's relation to the world is conceived on the pattern of the speculative intellect's ascent to divinity. God, as the first, cannot be said to be conceived directly in the image of human intellect, yet the way to God certainly is. The strategy is congenial even to Maimonides, who devotes an entire chapter to showing that God is understanding, the one understanding, and what is understood (1.68), after having shown that "on account of the divine intellect with which man has been endowed, he is said to have been made in the form and likeness of the almighty" (1.1). It is significant that Maimonides makes such an identification after having explicitly rejected positive attribution *in divinis*; the immediate source seems to be Ibn-Sina.[6] So the pull to adopt the model of speculative intellect for understanding God's relation to the world, and hence God's knowing, seems quite irresistable to philosophers. Moreover, as we shall see, that model will also determine the scope and extent of God's knowledge of the world.

Jewish, Christian, and Muslim insistence on creation, however, conspired to press for another analogy. This was readily available in Aristotle's division of knowing into speculative and practical—so much that one wonders that it was not seized on earlier. The predominance of the Neo-platonic synthesis, plus philosophy's consistent preference for speculative knowing (which could also be elaborated into a logic), witnessed in a writer as influential as Porphyry, conspire to explain the oversight.[7] In fact, one might add, language itself contributes to fastening on to speculative knowing as paradigmatic, even to the exclusion of practical knowing, for only examples of speculative knowing take the form 'I know that p'. Practical reasoning concludes not in a statement but in an action ("after some deliberation I called her") while the artist's activity results in an *opus*: "following your suggestion, here's what I made." So one has some notion of how difficult it will be to sustain a middle ground between intellectual emanation and sovereign will, even though the model of practical reason be available.

5.2   Towards Securing Creation

When one sets out to offer an account of creation, it turns out that a *beginning* is conceptually less crucial than total dependency on One. The creator, after all, could have created "from all eternity." Yet how could one distinguish a free act of One—not merely first in a scheme, but utterly first—without insisting that the world had a beginning? Such is the rhetorical force of a beginning, especially in the face of such convenient emanation schemes. What is at stake is "the distinction" of God from the world, and a glance at the early chapters of Alfarabi's *Ideas of the Inhabitants of the Virtuous City* will show how a discussion of "the first being" can so easily leave obscure what we found to be so central: one can read his text with or without accentuating "the distinction," and find it coherent either way.

Ibn-Sina's division of all that is into necessary and possible being, articulated by showing existence to be something additional to essence in all but the first being, would seem to have secured "the distinction" in a radical way. Yet, as has been noted, the form of his thought about the One also required that the world emanate from it with an eternal necessity. Part of the conception of necessary being is to emanate the first intelligence, from (and through) which everything else comes into being. The result is a universe determined in its being by the first (1.7, 47:10–15) yet in itself *false* (*batil*) (1.8, 48:8–10). This latter observation, bolstered by the celebrated Qur'anic verse: "everything perishes except his [God's] face" (28:88; also 55:26-7), plays upon the use of *haqiqa* (truth, reality) for essence (8.6, 356: 10–15). (Arabic stays close to common usage here, much as we would speak of the truth, or heart of the matter; the essence of it.) One might also wonder whether Ibn-Sina could not be heading off an "essentialism" which could ensue from his fastening upon existence as what each possible being receives from the One. He is explicit enough that matter alone is presupposed, as a pure possibility, so that everything can literally be said to proceed from necessary being: the permanent source of all that is, at each instant making created things exist in drawing them out of the void (*batil*).[8] Yet by exploiting the polyvalence of *haqiqa*—*true, real, or essence*—he can also underscore that everything is bestowed by the first.

Al-Kindi (c. 801–866) had already proposed another distinction: between "the true Agent [who] makes what he makes without being acted upon," and "everything beneath Him, i.e. all His creations, [who] are called agents in a metaphorical, not in the proper sense; because in the proper sense they are all acted upon."[9] Moreover "the kind of action [which] belongs properly to God, . . . i.e. action in the proper sense, is making existent existences from the non-existent" (*ta'yis al-aysat an lays*: a phrase constructed by al-Kindi to make just this point). This distinction is imbedded in an emanation scheme, so that "the first of [the agents (in a metaphorical sense)] is acted upon by the Creator, the rest by each other."

The distinction itself, of course, played directly into the hands of the religious thinkers who found themselves impelled to exalt God's activity by downgrading human responsibility.[10] Perhaps for this reason it was not developed by philosophical tradition, where it would also have suffered the fate of all distinctions which try to reduce the *prima facie* exemplary sense of a notion to a secondary role. (So 'agent', in its normal sense, would always need to be explicated as 'agent-in-a-metaphorical-sense'.) In any case, such a distinction could not fail to lead to unflattering consequences for the world in which we live—and for agents as we know and experience them ourselves.

Similarly for Ibn-Sina's bold assertion that things in themselves are false or empty. It is fair to say, of course, that he does not extract from that assertion the radical mystical consequences that will attract an al-Ghazali (see note 8), and that he could argue that we never encounter things "in-themselves," but always as determined to a manner of being, and as such they are real and true (*haqq*). The force of his negative assertion about things "in themselves," then, is not to make us re-assess the reality of the world we live in, but to invite us to discover the roots of its reality in the One. There is a mystical streak in Ibn-Sina, though it is less renunciating than monistic in tone. Yet that too threatens an adequate formulation of "the distinction'" as we have seen, even if it does not so directly question the status of created things.

Nevertheless, al-Kindi, Alfarabi, and Ibn-Sina have

provided the materials for a more satisfactory articulation of creation, and the relation of creator to everything else. By altering the Neoplatonic scheme where the One lies "beyond being" as the good to which all aspire, to identify the One with the "first being" (Alfarabi) or "necessary existence" (Ibn-Sina) from which comes all that exists, the stage is set for conceiving that relationship in a way which accentuates "the distinction" and can even dispense with the emanation scheme. The key to such a formulation, I have suggested, will be Aristotle's notion of practical reason, and the pivotal figure in moving towards it is Moses Maimonides.

We have noted how spontaneously Maimonides adopted Ibn-Sina's formulations for God as the One in whom "existence and essence are perfectly identical" (1.57). Yet when it came to characterizing the relation of that One to the universe, he demurred. For he found the arguments from causal necessity uncompelling (2.21) and the explanatory pretenses of the emanation scheme to exceed the evidence (2.19, 2.22). In short, he proposed another image, that of design (or purpose) opposing it to necessity (2.19), going on to insist that bringing together "existing in virtue of necessity and being produced in time in virtue of a purpose and a will . . . comes near to a combination of two contraries" (2.20 [Pines])—that is, the two positions are formally incompatible.

Once again, Maimonides has located the difference accurately: in the controlling metaphors and the way they either obscure or underscore "the distinction" of God from the world. Taking issue with "some of the recent philosophers" who try to combine the eternity of the universe with the assertion that God "by His will designs and determines its existence and form" (2.21), Maimonides accuses them of "abandoning the term 'necessary result', but retaining the theory of it." Unable to rise above a human conception of the relation between agent and product, they were reluctant to admit that creation took place "at one certain time," lest that imply potentiality in God. Maimonides responds that God "is always an actual agent," so to act at a certain time entails no move from potency to act in divinity (cf. 2.18). So it is critical to insist on a beginning, lest verbal patchwork obscure the incompatibility between these two positions. As Maimonides insists, "when we speak of design . . . we mean to express by it that the Universe is not the 'necessary result' of God's existence, as the effect is the necessary result of the efficient cause." As if to underscore that "the distinction" is at stake, he goes on to remind us: "in the latter case the effect cannot be separated from the cause" (1.21).

So the lines of demarcation are drawn, and the contrasting lines of thought clearly delineated: 'necessary result' versus 'design' or 'purpose'. Maimonides goes on to show how the first is embodied in the scheme of emanating intelligences, suggesting how it shows forth the necessity of speculative knowing in the logic of drawing conclusions.[11] Similarly, the language of design, purpose and will, summarizing as it does the language of the scriptures (2.30), introduces us into the realm of practical knowing. Maimonides does not explicitly invoke this distinction to mark the difference, but everything is in place to do so. Moreover, such a strategy would be in line with his own at this point: to eschew doing battle, as though one were in a position conclusively to prove either side (as the Muslim religious thinkers pretended to do [1.71]). Rather, to show that the view of "those who follow the law of Moses . . . that the whole Universe, i.e., everything except God, has been brought by Him into existence out of non-existence" (2.13), is not impossible; and can even be shown to be superior to the view Aristotle and others (including Ibn-Sina) proposed that "everything besides that [first] Being is the necessary result of [it]" (1.21).

Without, then, entering into Maimonides' arguments, I propose to capitalize on the precisions he has made to show how the distinction between speculative and practical knowing can advance our inquiry into the relation between God and the world. Moreover, it will also help to shift the scene from creation itself, on which Maimonides has little to say, to God's knowledge of individuals and of particular events. For all who accept Aristotle's focus on individuals as what primarily exists, the way we succeed or fail to characterize God's relation to primary existents will test our capacity to formulate the relationship. Moreover, as we shall see, Aquinas' elaboration of that knowledge will at once extend Maimonides' shaping metaphors and rejoin the issue of creation.

5.3   Maimonides and Ibn-Sina: A Shared Pattern

To ask about God's knowledge is to probe the relation of the first principle to all that comes from it, in an effort to understand the dependence more specifically. The question quickly becomes that of providence, in religious terms, since the first principle will not simply know but also care. Here is where the difference of these thinkers from Aristotle is so striking. For while Maimonides will cite for criticism Aristotle's view of providence (3.17), he can only mean the eternal regularity of the universe, which the first mover assures.[12] So his criticisms can mock the indifference of Aristotle's "God" to the fate of individuals, but that only shows how much the scene has shifted. For Aristotle's prime mover need not assume an *attitude* towards the world; indifference is not a privation with regard to it.[13] Ibn-Sina articulates the new situation in a neat formula:

> Because [necessary being] is the principle (*mabda*) of all being, it knows by its essence that of which it is the principle: beings perfect in their reality (*bi-a'yan*), and corruptible beings in their species but not in the midst of their individuality (*bi-ashkas*) (8.6, 359:1-2).

The first principle must know what comes forth directly

from it, for while emanation is necessary, it is not blind. What emanates directly from necessary being is, of course, the first intelligence, yet whatever follows from that primary emanation without any of the contingency associated with matter and corruptibility, will likewise be known by the first principle of all. The manifest pattern, we have noted, is that of logical consequence inherent in speculative knowledge, which makes the position persuasive in its coherence: God knows all there is to know.[14] For all that is knowable (in this fashion) of the individual is its specific character, nothing is missing thereby: "the individual thing does not escape what concerns [necessary being] on this account, as 'not so much as the weight of an ant in earth or heaven escapes from thy Lord' [Qur'an 10:61]" (8.6, 359:13-14).

The example which Ibn-Sina offers to illustrate that final point—that all that is knowable of an individual is its specific character—is that of a solar eclipse. His arguments come to persuading that one eclipse differs from another only in occurrence, so to know what an eclipse is, is in effect, to have seen them all. A plausible enough argument, yet it only confirms that everything turns on one's selection of a paradigm for 'individual'. By using an eclipse, Ibn-Sina moved in the direction of singulars as instances of secondary substances, while Maimonides takes issue with such an account by baldly insisting that "everything in real existence is an individual object" (3.18), so that to know what really exists will be to know it in its individuality and not as instantiating a species. Since his concern is particularly the relation between God and human beings, as presupposed in the Torah, his Aristotelian insistence is all the more understandable.

Yet before considering the modifications Maimonides must make to establish his contention that God cares for each individual human being, it would be well to appreciate the power of Ibn-Sina's position. While it clearly strains credibility to try to assimilate his theory with the sense of

the Qur'an regarding God's surveillance over creatures, it
does capture quite well the tenor of philosophers' discus-
sions of the matter as well as fairly widespread popular
belief. It corresponds to philosophers' predilections for the
speculative pattern of knowing, as reflected in logical consequences; and it translates widespread incredibility regarding God's really being interested in each one of us, into a
plausible scheme. Dubbed either 'stoicism' or 'deism', that
popular philosophy presumes an order to the universe, to
which human beings are counseled to adapt themselves. It
is generally thought to be reckless (or Nietzschean) to
flaunt it, though one cannot but admire the bravado of
those who try.

If this sounds more like Aristotle than like someone
struck by biblical or Qur'anic assertions of creation, that
would be a just assessment. Such reflections on order,
while often presuming a divinity, are quite compatible
with a weak form of deism, supplemented or not by a
pantheon of powers. So a more radical conceptual move
will have to be made to articulate the new status of beings-
as-created, and the unique position of the creator. "The
distinction" does not come naturally; it seems rather to be
subject to a kind of natural or inertial erosion.

Maimonides balks at the indifference to individuals of a
God whose influence (cf. 2.12) stops at "the preservation
of the species [so that] all other movements . . . made by
individual members of the species are due to accident"
(3.17). His examples are eloquent appeals to our sense for
the vast difference between "the falling of a leaf or a stone
and the death of good and noble people in a ship." He
does not single out Ibn-Sina for criticism, it is true; his target is Aristotle. Yet we have seen how vulnerable Ibn-Sina
would be to the same critique, and even more justly, since
such indifference would be a yawning privation in Ibn-
Sina's God, whose notice encompasses all, even to the
weight of an atom! Since Maimonides' concern is more
religious than philosophical at this point, he is content to

counterpose "our theory, or that of our law" to the coherently pagan position of Aristotle on the one hand, and the
mutually excluding Asharite and Motazalite schools of
Muslim thought on the other.

For the purposes of our story, however, Ibn-Sina's inability to achieve a closer rapproachment with the Qur'an
can be explained in philosophical terms as (1) a fixation on
the speculative pattern for knowing as elaborated in the
inherited emanation scheme, and (2) his inability to find a
proper ontological home for that existence which "comes
to" possible beings. As a result, he was led to betray his
own Aristotelian commitment to individual existing things
as primary beings, to treat them as *instances* of a kind. The
same displacement can be noted in the way in which he
makes the distinction of existence from essence, by concen-
trating on essences "in themselves"; it is more evident here
if we contrast his example of an eclipse with Maimonides'
concern for "Zaid"—the Arab equivalent of "Socrates."[15]
Maimonides' concern for the Torah (which Gersonides will
deride as "constraints") led him to question (1) Ibn-Sina's
fixation on the speculative model for knowing, without
however escaping its spell. It will take an Aquinas to make
the radical ontological moves needed to secure a proper
home for existence.

What Maimonides actually does is to assert that God
knows and cares for individual human beings. He does this
expressly with reference to two fundamental principles of
the law of Moses: that of "man's perfectly free will," and
that "wrong cannot be ascribed to God in any way whatever" (3.17). The gift of the Torah implies that those
receiving it be free to follow or spurn its injunctions, so
that the consequence of one or the other can rightly be
expected to be reward or punishment, respectively. Thus
"all evils and afflictions as well as all kinds of happiness
of man, whether they concern one individual person or
a community, are distributed according to justice." (So
neat a principle is challenged, of course, in the Bible itself

by the Book of Job, to which Maimonides will devote three later chapters: 3.22-24.) In the terms he has set for himself, this position assumes a high middle ground between Asharite denial of the intentional initiative proper to freedom and hence apparent attribution of evil (or at least extreme arbitrariness) to God, and the Motazalite extension of divine justice and recompense to a cosmic (and to his mind, comic) scale.

With regard to the scope of such providential care, however, Maimonides takes responsibility himself for restricting it to individual *human* beings. In advancing such a position, he relies not "on demonstrative proof, but on my conception of the spirit of the Divine Law, and the writings of the Prophets." (One suspects, indeed, that most believing Jews or Christians would find his view eminently sensible.) There can be no doubt, certainly, that the paradigm for an individual in the Bible is the same as in our ordinary parlance—a human being; and especially so in the Hebrew scriptures where they are the recipients of a divine address and call. And Maimonides is at pains to corroborate his conceptions from the scriptures. When it comes to describing how this care is administered, however, he betrays the power of the emanation scheme and its account of spheres of divine influence:

> I hold that Divine Providence is related and closely connected with the intellect, because Providence can only proceed from an intelligent being, from a being that is itself the most perfect intellect. Those creatures, therefore, which receive part of that intellectual influence, will become subject to the action of Providence in the same proportion as they are acted upon by the Intellect (3.17).

He does not bolster this view of the actual working of providence with regard to individual human beings from scriptural texts, though he does assert that it "is in accordance with reason and with the teaching of Scripture." One wonders, however, how it would square with prophetic urgings that "God desires not the death of the sinner but that he be converted and live," especially as these are embodied in the God of Hosea who would recall Israel to the desert and there speak to her heart. It sounds rather like those will be cared for who participate in the divine order, and to the extent that they conform to that "intellectual influence" already explicated (2.12) in terms of the emanation scheme. Everyone else, it is implied, will be "left to their own devices." Moreover, the contention "that Divine Providence is in each case proportional to the person's intellectual development" finds corroboration in Alfarabi's *Commentary on Aristotle's Nichomachean Ethics*: "Those who possess the faculty of raising their souls from virtue to virtue obtain, according to Plato, Divine protection to a higher degree" (2.18).

One might have thought Aristotle's corroboration to be less than desirable in this case, given the touted indifference of his "God" to individuals. Although Maimonides treats it as one of those serendipitous confirmations by pagan thinkers of the Law of Moses, he does so not when treating the principles of that Law, but in the presentation of his conception of its spirit—and indeed, of a description of its working. A more impartial reader could just as well take this coincidence with Aristotle, and indeed his virtual resumption of the emanationist "mysticism" of Ibn-Sina, as a sign of entrapment in a model for knowing that is univocally speculative and hence leaves no real room for a creator.[16] Such a criticism would be confirmed by the final chapter of the *Guide,* where the "true perfection of man" is equated with "true metaphysical opinions [beliefs] as regards God" (3.54). Where will there be room to introduce a new model for God's knowing and hence for the relation of creator to creation?

5.4   *Knowing as Making and Doing*

By way of acknowledging the force of Ibn-Sina's position regarding God's knowledge of individuals, Maimonides attempts to locate it in the unwitting presumption "that God's knowledge is like ours" (3.20). Moreover, philosophers are most to be blamed for such a howler, since they had already "demonstrated that there is no plurality in God, and that He has no attribute that is not identical with His essence; His knowledge and His essence are one and the same thing . . . , that our intellect and our knowledge are insufficient to comprehend the true idea of His essence" (3.20). Given these shared convictions, how can they presume to assimilate God's knowledge to ours, when—as identical with God's essence—"His knowledge is not of the same kind as ours, but totally different from it and admitting of no analogy?" So we rejoin Moses' original contention regarding perfections we find ourselves attributing to God: there can be no way of understanding them "positively." Indeed, Gersonides will presume that it is the pressures generated by the "constraints of the Torah" and an accepted notion of knowledge—especially Maimonides' concern that "God's knowledge of one of two eventualities . . . not determine it"—which actually drove him to his agnostic position on divine attributes.[17]

Whatever be the explanation, the position is an intrinsically unstable one, yet responds to a keen philosophical and religious instinct countering any attempts to confine the relation of creator to creation to an emanation scheme pattern on logical consequence. Both instinct and instability are displayed in his summary statement:

> As there is an Essence of independent existence, which is, as the philosophers call it, the Cause of the existence of all things, or, as we say, the Creator of everything that exists beside Him, so we also assume that this Essence knows everything, that nothing whatever of all

that exists is hidden from it [allusion to Qur'an 20:61?], and that the knowledge attributed to this essence has nothing in common with our knowledge, just as that essence is in no way like our essence (3.20).

The similarities and differences with Ibn-Sina are all in place, and admirably so, yet if that were Maimonides' final statement on the matter, he would himself be as tripped up by the expressed "homonymity of the term 'knowledge'" as he contends it has misled others. For what could we then make of his insistence that "this Essence *knows* everything?" Fortunately, his own gloss on the matter in the following chapter attenuates the claim of radical disanalogy by offering a model for locating the crucial difference between the creator's knowing and a creature's.

"There is a great difference between the knowledge which the producer of a thing possesses concerning it, and the knowledge which other persons possess concerning the same thing" (3.21). These words introduce the model of the artisan for divine knowing. After elaborating the case of a clock, and the difference of viewpoint between its designer and one inspecting it, he concludes: "the same is the case with every object, and its relation to our knowledge and God's knowledge of it." The principle which he draws from this difference enunciates a fully intentional activity of creation: "His knowledge of things is not derived from the things themselves; if this were the case, there would be change and plurality in His knowledge; on the contrary, the things are in accordance with His eternal knowledge. . . . He fully knows His unchangeable essence, and has thus a knowledge of all that results from any of His acts" (3.21).

The principle will be adopted whole-cloth by Aquinas, as we shall see, who will also use it to dispense with all vestiges of an emanation scheme. His expressed reason will be that nothing created can possibly have a share in that power which belongs to the Creator alone; we can well see him removing all traces of a speculative model for articulating the creator-creation relationship. In that sense, he would be responsive to the spirit of Maimonides' claims of radical disanalogy with *speculative* knowing; an interpretation strengthened by Maimonides' comments on his final statement, regarding God's knowing God's own essence and all that results from any diverse act: "If we were to try to understand in what manner this is done, it would be the same as if we tried to be the same as God, and to make our knowledge identical with His Knowledge." For even the artisan analogy expressly denies in the case of God what every artist takes great care to select: a pre-existing material.

Yet Maimonides leaves the subject, simply recommending the artisan analogy: "for I think that this is an excellent idea, and leads to correct views; no error will be found in it; no dialectical argument; it does not lead to any absurd conclusion, nor to ascribing any defect to God" (3.21). High praise indeed from one whose fear of ascribing any positive attribute to God finally rested on his concern to avoid any hint of *idolatry*, however unintended or even well-meant (1.59). Since Maimonides is not composing a systematic theology, but rather alerting Joseph to ways in which an attendant philosophy may hinder or help one's appropriation of the Torah, he can leave the subject once he has suggested an analogy for divine knowing that will not prove misleading, and warned his readers away from expecting any assistance at all from current schemes for speculative knowing. It is significant for our story that Aquinas takes up just where Maimonides left off.

It is true, of course, that Western thinkers were less beholden to emanation schemes in their attempts to grasp the relation between God and the world. The Christological controversies had already rendered them suspect, and by rejecting the philosophically more plausible Arian alternative, the West opted at once for an uncreated procession within divinity and for a union between divine and human natures in Christ that left them "distinct and unmixed" in one acting person. "The distinction" between God and the world, then, could be formulated the more precisely when confronted with one who purported to unite them in his person. For the proclamation of their unity in Jesus believed to be the Christ at once demanded clarity about their distinctness, especially in the person of the Word-made-flesh, and also tempered any fears that insisting on "the distinction" would have the effect of removing God from God's world. The doctrine of incarnation assured the strongest possible connection. [18]

Augustine had already neutralized eternal or "necessary truths" by giving them due place "in the mind of God."[19] And Aquinas went a step further to insure that God need not consult them, as it were, in creating, by insisting that such ideas should be thought of in God "not as that *by which* the thing to be made was understood," as though they supplied the "form making the [divine] intellect to be in act" (*ST* 1.15.2). Rather, "insofar as God knows the divine essence as *so imitable* by such a creature, God knows it [divine essence] *as* the proper *ratio* and idea of this creature." That is, the necessary truths attendant upon creation neither have eternal status independent of God's creative intent, nor are they themselves created (as Descartes arguably opined). Rather, their necessity, and hence their claim to atemporality, are precisely attendant upon God's creative intent, since they represent the diverse manners in which the divine essence may be "imitable" in creation. This maneuver, as we shall see, completed the process of "de-platonizing" begun by Augustine, and rendered any emanation scheme quite redundant.

For Aquinas' demonstration that God must know singulars explicitly sets itself against Avicenna's position (communicated to him in al-Ghazali's summary reported in Averroes *Tahafut* 6.9), by distinguishing the mode proper to "divine knowledge of things, [which] is to be compared to the knowledge of an artisan, since it is the cause of all things as art is [the cause] of artifacts" (*De ver.* 2.5). It is this difference above all which sets God's knowledge apart from ours: "the similitude of the things" which we attain by abstraction "is only a similitude of [its] form, while the similitude of the thing in the divine intellect is productive of the thing (*factiva rei*)." Moreover, that "similitude," which is none other than the divine essence, can be "the similitude of the thing with respect to what is proper to the thing itself (and so be its proper *ratio*) . . . according as each thing imitates it in diverse ways" (*De ver.* 2.4.2). "In this way," Aquinas says, "the divine essence makes (*facit*) a proper knowledge of each thing, insofar as it is the proper *ratio* of each one" (ibid.).

Aquinas manages to re-affirm Ibn-Sina's fundamental contention that necessary being, in knowing its essence knows all that emanates from it (8.6), yet by shifting the mode of knowing from speculative to practical, not only extends God's knowing to singulars, but grants it an intentionality *par* excellence: God knows the particular manner in which each individual participates in the divine essence, and so can be said to know the *ratio* proper to each thing— "indeed the singular essence of each individual" (*De ver.* 2.7). We shall see in a moment how Aquinas is able to speak of 'individual essence' without postulating anything like Scotus' *haecceitas*; at this point it is well to note how his treatment also underscores Maimonides' concern that divine knowing not simply be assumed to be like ours (3.20).

The radical disparity between the two knowings follows from the difference in mode: "our knowledge is derived from things and hence naturally posterior to them, while the knowledge the Creator has of creatures (and the artisan of artifacts) naturally precedes the things known. [As a result] God's knowledge and ours have the opposite orientation [*habitudo*] to the things known" (*De ver.* 2.8). The *Summa* resumes this point in an arresting image: "natural things are midway between God's knowledge and ours— ours being derived from those things of which God's is the cause" (1.14.8.3). So any comparison between the two knowings must be made most judiciously, as Aquinas' deft performance continually shows, underscored by the care with which he proposed drawing acceptable analogies between the two (*De ver.* 2.11). It would hardly be rash to consider Aquinas proceeding in the spirit of Maimonides, in adopting the artisan model which he expressly commends, and in using it to accentuate the vast difference between knowing *in divinis* and among us.

How can Aquinas so formulate the relation between creator and creature as to assure so intimate a knowledge of individuals, and do so without postulating that curious hybrid, an "individual essence"? In other words, how does he put the artisan model for knowing to use in framing a metaphysical scheme adequate to God's being the creator for each individual? To answer these questions we must turn to Aquinas' explicit treatment of creation, where his identification of *esse* as "the effect proper to the first and most universal cause, which is God" (*ST* 1.45.5) will allow him to articulate the relationship of creator to creatures without recourse to any emanation scheme, and hence free of any reference to a speculative model for knowing. This is the full step into a creationist ontology, for which Ibn-Sina prepared the way by insisting that existence (*wujud*) be distinct from essence (*mahiyya*). His predilection for the speculative model for knowing, however, as embodied in the emanation scheme inherited from Alfarabi, would impede him from such a step. Maimonides suggested and strongly commended another model for knowing, that of "the producer of a thing," yet remained enough in the sway of the speculative emanation account to forbear drawing its consequences. Moreover, the step Aquinas took would also require clarifying the status of that *existence* which Ibn-Sina had distinguished; and while Maimonides capitalizes upon the distinction to formulate divinity as the One in which "existence and essence are perfectly identical" (1.57), he is content to rest with Ibn-Sina's less than adequate treatment of the matter. So the final chapter in this story also involves a moment of genuine philosophical creativity.

6. Eternal Creator of
Contingent Things

THE BETTER TO ILLUSTRATE Aquinas' way of articulating
God's being the creator of each individual, it would be well
once again to appreciate the power of Alfarabi's emanation
scheme. What appears at first to a modern reader as a gratuitous exercise in "science fiction" turns out to offer a
plausible way of elaborating the relation between the first
principle and all else. For it embodies the perennial attrac-
tion of Platonism: an intellectual mysticism whereby we
can ascend to a fine point of unified light which lies beyond
articulation, certainly, yet confirms the order we have
discovered, allowing us to put our hope in it. That sense of
cosmic order, translating the influence of the Good according to definite levels of understanding, seems to have inspired the emanation scheme. So one might be willing to
attenuate its causal pretensions to derive the benefits of
such an order. And if we add to it Maimonides' healthy
dose of human freedom, so as to avoid dilemmas of divine
responsibility for evil, we may be said to have formulated a
general attitude towards creation and providence shared
by most sensible religious people—Jews, Christians, or
Muslims. (Making allowances, withal, for the peculiar role
some Christians reserve for "sacraments," as well as Muslim
sensitivity about God's overriding presence to human
destiny.)

Yet something is missing in that widespread and sensible religious attitude, or those same traditions would never have spawned prophets or mystics. And what is missing is precisely the sense of God's intimate presence to each individual. It simply will not do to affirm creation and then let it degenerate into a deism indistinguishable from a necessary emanation of a first principle. Nor will it do to affirm a special providence for human beings, as Maimonides did, but then go on to elucidate it in terms congenial to the intellectual mysticism of an Ibn-Sina. Yet the power of the sensible attitude reasserts itself the moment we try to think about God's creating and conserving individual things, especially when we add a good dose of chance—luck, good and bad. And where are we to begin counting individuals? A single leaf?[1]

What we realize, however, when we begin such imaginings, is that we are presuming a computer-like inventory on the part of God, as though things were objects for God as they are for us. The next step would be to imagine possible trajectories, as though providence were a cosmic form of game-theory. So we have fulfilled Maimonides' fears by unwittingly presuming God's knowledge to be like ours. And the sign that we have done so is our recourse to the speculative model for knowing, as though God were monitoring the world. But the master-image of creator already suggests an analogy with practical reason, and Maimonides counseled that only the consistent application of such an analogy will guide our thinking properly in these regions (3.21).

6.1   Aquinas' Account of Creation

So Aquinas' treatment builds upon the assertion that "God's knowledge is indeed the cause of things: for the knowledge of God is related to [*se habet ad*] all created things as the knowledge of an artisan is related to artifacts"

(*ST* 1.14.8). That principle is then elaborated in the questions devoted to creation in terms of the distinction he has drawn between essence and *esse* (existence). Creating belongs to God alone, because what we mean by 'creation' is the "emanation of all *esse* from the universal being" (*ST* 1.45.4.1), or alternatively, "the emanation of all being (*entis*) from the universal cause, which is God" (1.45.1). (He uses the term 'emanation' in this context deliberately, since 'production' [which he also uses—1.45.4.3] tends to presume a material cause, and the points at issue here are *creatio ex nihilo* and creation without intermediaries. He also does not hesitate to use the term 'cause', since his earlier treatment on God's knowledge (*ST* 1.15) already insured that the causation is a thoroughly intentional exercise of practical reason.) And since God alone is "subsistent *esse* itself" (*ST* 1.44.1), only God can be the "principle of *esse* insofar as it is *esse* [i.e., the to-be of each existing thing]" (*De pot.* 3.4, *ST* 1.45.5.1).

Here we have the heart of Aquinas' treatment. Ibn-Sina's distinction of necessary from possible being, as that whose very essence was to-be, implied that everything but necessary being was "composed" of essence and existence. Aquinas refined *wujud*, which could be translated as *ens* or as *esse* as the act of being (*actus essendi*). This allowed him to formulate God's unity unequivocally (as we have seen) as that one whose essence is simply to-be; and using the same distinction, to identify *esse* as "the effect proper to the first and most universal cause, which is God" (*ST* 1.45.5). So the same principle which can formulate divine unity can also adequately articulate "the distinction," since it is *esse* which gives to each individual its actuality as an existing thing.

Moreover, since "*esse* itself is the most common effect [of God], first and more intimate [to each thing] than all other effects, it belongs to God alone according to its peculiar power [*secundam virtutem propriam*]" (*De pot.* 3.7). So in giving each individual thing its existence, God may be said to be intimately present to each. From there it is a short step to maintain that "everything falls under divine providence, not merely in its universality but in its particularity" (*ST* 1.22.2). For "the causality of God, who is first agent, extends to all beings, not only to the principles of the species, but to the individual principles, not only to incorruptible things but also to corruptible. Whence it follows necessarily that all things which in any way have *esse*, are ordered to God as to their end." He is responding explicitly to Maimonides in this article, and does so by involving *esse* as the effect proper to God and most intimate to each existing thing, and closes by reminding us that God's "knowledge is to be compared to things as the knowledge of art to artifacts—hence everything comes under God's order as all artifacts fall under the order of art."

All need for an emanation scheme to transmit divine influence through unchanging entities to species, and thence to individuals as instances of them, is rendered otiose by identifying *esse* as at once the act of existence proper to each being and the proper effect of the creator's action, and rendering that activity on the model of practical knowing or art. Moreover, Aquinas is careful to note that such an interior presence of a properly divine effect in thngs does not jeopardize their integrity as existing individuals, and especially in what best manifests individuality: their proper agency. In an elaborate argument contending with the Islamic religious thinkers (*mutakallimun*), whose positions come to his attention through Maimonides, Aquinas concludes: from the fact that God "is within each thing not as part of its essence, but as maintaining the thing in *esse*, it follows that God operates immediately in any agent, without removing thereby the operation of intellect or will" (*De pot.* 3.7).

So the Aristotelian insistence that existing individuals offer the paradigm for *what is*, is given appropriate expression in Aquinas' use of *esse*, which also links each thing to its creator. And as I have suggested (2.3), that activity which Aquinas takes *esse* to be can best be understood by analogy with the act of judgment wherby we acknowledge a statement to be true. This would further succeed in elaborating Aristotle's account, for whom the primary orientation of 'is' remains that of ascertaining that something *is* the case.[2] Moreover, to think of *esse,* the "act of existing," on the model of the act of asserting something to be the case, also restores the element of *action* to speculative knowing by reminding us of its point: to discover what is the case. As Aristotle presumed the fact of things' existing, so he tended to conflate proposition with assertion, as declarative sentences naturally do. (When J. L. Austin began by distinguishing *illocutionary* force of statements from their merely locutionary component, he had to finish by wondering whether any statement could be purely "locutionary."[3])

So Aquinas' distinction of essence from *esse* can be recognized in the difference between considering a state of affairs and asserting it to be the case, or (in Aquinas' words) between the articulation of a thought in subject/predicate terms and the judgment of its truth. These reflections allow us to rejoin Aquinas to correct a potentially misleading consequence of insisting on contrasting the models of practical versus speculative knowing. The fact that the *mode* of God's knowledge of created things is to be understood as that of an artisan, so that God's knowledge naturally precedes the things which we then come to know, does not thereby deprive God of speculative knowledge. For, Aquinas insists, "an artisan has a *two-fold* knowledge of the thing-to-be-made: *speculative and practical*" (*De ver.* 2.8). For artisans first know what they want to make, and such knowledge becomes practical only when the artisan "intentionally extends the *rationes* of the work to be the goal of acting [*ad operationis finem*]" (ibid.). The practical knowing involved in making is then conceived as "being realized by an extension of the speculative to the work," so that the conclusion of such an act of knowing is the work itself.

The scenario, then, is a thoroughly practical one—creating the universe; it is simply that all practical knowing has its speculative component as well. The situation becomes that much more "speculative," however, when one wonders about those things which have not, are not, and will not come into being, yet which he wants to say God knows (*intuitur*) in the divine power, or as Aquinas prefers, "in divine goodness" (ibid). What about such "things"? Aquinas wants explicitly to save the term 'idea' for those which serve as *exemplars* of "whatever will come to be from God in any time" (*ST* 1.15.3, *De ver.* 3.3), and use *ratio* or 'similitude' for whatever "God knows as not to-be-produced by God's own self, so that the knowledge is purely speculative" (*De ver.* 3.3.2 [2nd series]). In the process of making these precisions, he even calls into question his own master contrast of speculative with practical understanding as a matter of "the forms deriving *from* things or of being [oriented] to things" (*De ver.* 3.3.5). For artisans can derive their forms from things by initiating another's product, and some speculative ideas can simply be dreamed up, or represent formal innovations, and so not all such ideas need be said to derive from things.

Yet while it is salutary to watch Aquinas raise cogent objections to his master contrast, they do not keep him from retaining it as the structural centerpiece of his creation account. And rightly so, for if the distinction is not an adequate one it is nonetheless pertinent to the case at hand. And we can see how by asking ourselves in what God's speculative knowing consists. Since the setting remains practical, oriented to creation, the answer has to be that God knows what God will or will not bring into being. (I am using 'will' in the intentional sense, of a piece with future action for us, but absent such connotations in an eternal creator.) Or, to put it more explicitly: "God knows some things, ordering them in such a way as they will be at some time, and of these [God] has actual practical knowledge; whereas God knows some things which at no time does [God] intend to make . . . , and of these God has a certain actual knowledge, but only virtually and not actually practiced knowledge" (*De ver.* 3.3).

From all this Aquinas concludes that God's "knowledge of things to-be-made (*operabilis*) by God includes the manner in which some are not to be made" (ibid.). That is, God knows which things God intends to bring into being and which things God does not so intend. That admission, however, does not license us to picture creation as God inspecting a number of possible scenarios to determine which one to bring into being. Nor need we trouble ourselves canvassing *all* that God knows without intending to bring it into being. The vision of a potential infinity of arrangements boggles the mind. All that Aquinas wishes to secure is that God's practical knowing which issues in creating the world we know bears sufficient analogies with artistry as we know it. Alternative designs remain a penumbra, or virtual part of an artist's creative act of making.

We can clarify this point, and also confirm the original master contrast, by asking how one might formulate the fact that God knows what God intends to bring into being and what God does not so intend: the first by a knowledge at once speculative and practical, the second by a knowledge that is purely speculative and only virtually practical. It would be misleading, certainly, to formulate the speculative component in propositional terms—as God knowing, for example, *that* the world is so structured as to respect the integrity of natural causes. It is strictly speaking false, of course, to imply that God knows *propositionally*, as though divine knowing were discursive and cumulative. But respecting that "formal feature" of divine cognition, and also respecting our need to formulate God's knowing on some analogy with our own, the properly qualified statement that God knows that-p (i.e., that the world is so structured . . .) remains severely misleading.

The reason harkens back to Aquinas' leading contrast
between God's knowledge and ours, deriving from the
thoroughly practical context of a creator's knowing. The
propositional (that-p) form is reserved for statements
about the world, either basic to one's worldview or
hypotheses to be confirmed. They convey, in other words,
a "knowledge derived from things." We would not even
say of ordinary artisans that they knew that the object
they crafted was of such a shape or form, as though that
were something they had to find out! We might ask them,
in the process, whether they knew *what* they were making,
and their customary answer would corroborate Aquinas'
account of the speculative component in making. They
would be able to give a description of *what* they were up
to, but it would be of a different sort than the critics'
assessment, itself inevitably framed in propositional terms.

The only propositional way to put *what* artisans know is
to say that they know that they are making, say, a likeness
of Sadat. The speculative knowing is utterly at the service
of the practical. Analogously, we can say: God knows that
God intends the world to be so structured as to respect the
integrity of natural causes. But that simply calls one's
attention to the fact that God's activity, like the artisans',
is conscious and intentional: God knows what God is
doing. That is all there is to it, and Aquinas means to say
no more in his qualification of the master contrast to
include a speculative component in God's knowing. Our
contention can be tested in a classic conundrum: God's
knowing of future contingent things and events. No treatment of divine knowledge of particulars can avoid grasping the nettle.

6.2   A Test Case: Future Contingencies

Before considering Aquinas on future contingents, it is
well to recall that the question need not arise for Ibn-Sina,

since God's knowledge comprehends individuals in their universality and not in their contingency, thus knowing all that is knowable about them. It had to arise for Maimonides, who asserted: "according to the teaching of our law, God's knowledge of one of two eventualities does not determine it, however certain that knowledge may be concerning the future occurence of the one eventuality" (3.20). This feature of God's knowledge offers the capital reason why "our knowledge . . . has only the name in common with God's knowledge." In other words, Maimonides left the issue unresolved, positing an intractable difference between divine and human uses of 'knowledge'. Yet since his own exposition in fact required a plausible sense of statements concerning God's knowing, he proved neither consistent nor helpful to Joseph on this question.

So Aquinas begins by taking issue with anyone who might presume, wittingly or unwittingly, to affirm that God knows what will happen; or as Maimonides put it: that God has "certain . . . knowledge . . . concerning the future occurence of one eventuality." "It would be impossible," Aquinas asserts, "for God to have knowledge of future contingents, were God to know them as future" (*De ver.* 2.12). For to know something to be the case is to ascertain that "it so obtains as it is apprehended," so knowledge of what does not yet exist is quite impossible. So if God is to know all things, "it would be better to say that God knows this thing to be, than that God knows 'the future', because to God things are never future but always present. . . . For that reason, God's knowledge of future things is more properly called 'providence' than 'pre-vidence'."

So the formal feature of God's eternity allows Aquinas to solve the logical dilemmas attending God's omniscience and contingency (especially freedom), since it allows him to deny that an "order of past to future" obtains "between divine knowledge and any contingent thing, but rather that the order of divine knowledge to anything is always like

the order of one present to a present thing." It is in that
sense, then, that "divine knowledge can be said to be related
to future contingencies as our eyes are related to the contingent things present to them" (*De malo* 16.7.15). For
the certainty of sense knowledge does not regard the form,
about which it can be misled, but the fact. Not that God
"*sees* the future," either, but that whatever was, is, or will
be is present to God's eternity "in its presentness [*presen-
tialitate*]" (*ST* 1.14.13), and thus known to be the case.

Aquinas readily acknowledges "the difficulty with this
position: that we cannot signify divine knowledge unless it
be after the manner of our knowing, attending at the same
time [*consignificando*; var.: *magnificando*] to the differences" (*De ver.* 2.12). Invoking the formal feature of
eternity can only magnify the disparity between divine and
human knowing, since our perspectives and our languages
are invariably tensed. Moreover, arguing the case for an
eternal divinity would distract us from this account.[4] Yet
the observations already made about the primarily practical
mode of God's knowing, and the consequent inappropriate-
ness of propositional formulae to convey it, may at least
help to dissolve dilemmas which arise from casting God's
knowledge of contingent things and events in terms of
propositions which God knows to be true. Correlative
questions attending a purported *scientia media* can be
dealt with similarly, as we shall see.

The speculative component of the creator's knowledge
to things-to-be-made is best formulated: God knows what
God intends to do. (Moreover, as with any artisan, this
involves a virtually practical and purely speculative understanding of what one does not intend it to do—not be
confused with attempting to conjure an infinity of arrangements which one intends *not* to do.) Since we are concerned
here with what will be rather than what will never take
place, such knowledge can be affirmed to be "productive
of the thing" [*factiva rei*] (*De ver.* 2.5), and hence "naturally precede the things known" (*De ver.* 2.8). So even if

the formal feature of divine eternity requires that whatever God knows be eternally present to God, as an object seen is present to our eyes, the master contrast must prevail. The thing which God knows is present to God as coming into being by divine creative action, while whatever certainty sense-knowledge has regarding things derives from the things' presence to our eyes.

So we can see once again how misleading it would be to formulate even the speculative component of God's creative knowing propositionally, as God's knowing *that* certain facts obtain regarding this individual. For God, as its creator, need not ascertain what is the case, and *ascertaining* is precisely what propositional language implies (or better, presupposes). This argument is more persuasive, the more one recognizes the role judgment plays in ascertaining that something indeed "obtains as it is apprehended" (*De ver.* 2.12)—a key ingredient in Aquinas' epistemology and crucial to his treatment of this question. Yet however much philosophies of a broadly "platonist" bent tend to elide judgment to speak of 'true propositions', even they must admit that we don't just *find* them! Moreover, the difference which the master contrast forcibly draws between making something to be (true) and ascertaining whether what we say is indeed the case, can hardly be gainsaid. Aquinas' celebrated picture, then, of "natural things [suspended] halfway between God's knowledge and ours" (*ST* 1.14.8.3), assures that one not conflate the "truth of things" with our judgment of the truth of statements about them.[5]

Yet if we are not to confuse the "truth of things" (sometimes called "metaphysical truth") with *truth* as we ordinarily use the term (with reference to our assertions), how are they to be related? We are tempted to say, as two perspectives on natural things, yet that locution slights the master contrast, presuming the creator also to have a "viewpoint." It helps to recall that the very expression "truth of things" makes little sense unless we affirm creation (or emanation). For otherwise, things are; how could they be said to be true? Our statements may be true or false, but certainly not things themselves. Yet what God creates *can* be said to be true, as the result of God's creative knowing: practical in intent yet possessed of an appropriately speculative component.

Yet it would be odd and misleading, once again, to formulate that sense of a thing's being true as a true proposition which God knows—or better, as a proposition which God knows to be true. For we are dealing with another sort of knowing (practical, even creative) and hence with a clearly other sense of 'true'. In fact, what this sense of something's being true conveys is not merely its being *so,* but its *being so.* For God's practical knowing brings it into being as the sort of thing which we will (with some luck) ascertain it to be. So the master contrast is once again both confirmed and made operative by attending to *esse* as "the effect most proper to the first and most universal cause, which is God" (*ST* 1.45.5). In granting each thing its act of existing, God makes it to be, and its relation to its divine exemplar can then be called its truth.

Contingent events and things, then, which have not yet come to pass (so-called 'future contingents'), cannot be said to be known (in God's mind, as it were) *before* they come to pass, because they do not yet exist. God's eternal understanding of them in an exemplary fashion is ever ordered to God's intending them to exist at a certain time. The discrepancy between that time and God's eternity remains opaque to us, for it concerns the very mode of divine being. (That is what is meant by calling eternity a "formal feature" of divinity.) One can be helped a bit to respect that mystery be attending as we have to the master contrast in modes of knowing, and perhaps by Aquinas' pregnant remark that "eternity is the measure of enduring *esse* [*permanentis*] as time is the measure of change

[*motus*]" (*ST* 1.10.4). For the logical fact that whatever
exists, exists now, offers some paradoxical grasp of *esse*,
by reminding us that what from one point of view is eva-
nescent, is also all we have!

6.3   Alternative Views of Contingency

The relations between time and eternity, however,
genuinely defy formulation, for the reasons we have noted.
One cannot say for that reason, however, that it is incoherent to speak of an eternal God. The fact that we cannot
formulate a relationship argues its transcendence, not its
incoherence. Explicit attempts to bridge that gap, however,
like *scientia media*, can be shown to be incoherent. For the
knowledge they demand that God have, on the one hand
of what might have taken place but does not, and on the
other of what has not yet come to pass, presuppose a
determinateness to the object known which only existence
could bestow. Hence those who propose such a knowledge
on God's part must also presume such arguable "entities"
as "individual natures" (*haecceitas*).[6] For if it is only *esse*
which grants an existing individual to be the individual it
is, then God cannot know such an individual apart from
granting it to be.

A view of freedom as selecting among alternatives apparently contributes to requiring the sort of knowledge posited
by *scientia media* if God's creation is to be a free and fully
intentional act. But other and more acceptable views of
freedom can account for one's freely deciding to marry
one's spouse without having to regard the action as selecting among a field. In fact, the more interior one's view of
freedom becomes, the more one can understand Aristotle's
observation that we are able to do the inevitable either
willingly or unwillingly (*N. Ethics* 3.1 [1110a 5-20]). In
any case, it would seem jejune to presume, without further
analysis, that God's freedom in creating would be given adequate expression by a mere freedom of choice. Moreover,

Aquinas' sense of a penumbra of things which God does not intend to bring into being would convey enough of that notion to assure that God's activity be free, without having to picture God canvassing alternatives.

It is this final feature of the *scientia media* scenario which suggests how inappropriate it is so to articulate the relation of creator to creation. For it appears to have reversed Aquinas' clear subordination of speculation to practical knowing in God as creator, to place the emphasis on the divine capacity for knowing what would happen were an arrangement of one sort or another to be brought into being. Besides the fatal blunder of pretending to know an individual where there is none to be known, this model accords to such speculative considerations the reason why God actualizes this rather than another "world." We have replaced a knowledgeable artisan with an all-seeing observer who finally acts. The intimacy of God to the world, which follows from Aquinas' bestower of *esse* to each individual, is given up in favor of a "decision tree" with a potential infinity of branches constituted by subjective conditionals: if x were . . . then y would be. . . . Some are drawn to such a treatment of God's knowledge because they cannot countenance Aquinas' expressly inexpressible relation of eternity to time. Some even imagine that an eternal God must be aloof from human affairs, and so prefer a scheme which conceives of God as knowing what will happen from within a temporal perspective, as a grand master in game theory. If the master contrast which Aquinas draws be taken as the primary axiom, however, and divine eternity be understood for what it is—a formal feature of divinity as such—then the creator who bestows *esse* and is hence present to each moment of time as it exists in its respective *now* will be one intimately engaged with each individual. And when such individuals are intentional beings, capable of knowing and loving, such a God will be responsive to them as they are responsive to divine promptings. Nor does such a picture in any way clash with another formal feature of divinity—unchangeableness—since intentional interaction is not change but involves the responsiveness of knowing and loving.[7]

One might put it in the following way: while an eternal God at first appearance is outside of time and hence removed from history, a closer look at Aquinas' manner of articulating such a God's relation to the world suggests just the opposite. For the creator, whose "knowledge of created things [is to be understood] after the manner in which the artisan knows artifacts" (De ver. 2.8), knows each thing in a manner which involves bringing it into being, and hence "in the manner in which each one of them is an act in itself" (ST 1.14.13). And since the difference between accounts of existing individuals and those of "possible worlds" is precisely what divides history from scenarios for possible action, Aquinas' formulation stands a better chance of articulating the God of history in whom Jews, Christians, and Muslims believe, than those whose knowledge of the world involves abstract counterfactuals. The expressly inexpressible relation of eternity to time is rendered metaphorically by Aquinas, as "eternity embracing all of time" (1.14.3). The recourse to metaphor marks the limits of language, and the negative component in the affirmation that this God gives to each thing its to-be. For nothing less than an eternal creator could be so intimately present to each existing thing, as the way of expressing divine transcendence more congenial to the speculative model for knowledge will, it seems, require either an emanation scheme or counterfactual scenarios.

So everything can be seen to turn on our capacity to conceive Ibn-Sina's distinction of existence from essences in a way which allows esse to be the act of existence of each individual. The suggested analogy for grasping the notion "act of existence" is the judgment whereby we ascertain that a proposed assertion is not only coherent but true. For true cannot be located as a property of statements any more than esse conceived as an accident of things, since neither represents a quality said of statement or thing, respectively. Each rather expresses the fact that a proposal entertained may in fact be asserted, on the one hand; or that an object under consideration in fact exists. To expound the two notions together shows how structurally parallel they are, and also allows them to be presented as an explicitation of what Aristotle left presupposed in his treatment of statements, and indeed in his overall elucidation of *beings* as "what is (the case)."[8]

Ibn-Sina's preliminary identification of existence (*wujud*) as what "comes to" essence, was vulnerable to the criticism of Ibn-Rushd and others on two counts: (1) its apparent ontological location as an accident ran counter to the grammar as of accident of being "in another," namely substance, whose subsistence was presumed; and (2) accidents are said of things, not of essences. Yet his critics missed the more pertinent point of the distinction: to attempt to characterize the contingency of all created things. Ibn-Rushd, especially, by affirming Aristotle's presumption of a world of being, simply reinforced the classical scheme without sensing Ibn-Sina's opening to an utterly new sense of *contingency*. In locating existence as *esse*, the act of existing, Aquinas discovered an appropriate idiom for that dependency of all from the creator as the source of its being, which is the heart of the new sense of contingency.

We have also noted that Ibn-Sina was unable to formulate this relationship for yet another reason: his predilection for the speculative model for knowing, embodied in an emanation scheme reflecting logical consequence. So everything that is emanates from the first principle, yet necessarily so (as consequences follow from conclusions), at least with respect to its universal characteristics. Beyond that lie the intractable contingencies of matter. Aquinas, perhaps assisted by Maimonides, altered the model for knowing to arrive at a free and creative act of God at the source of all things. This model, together with the clearer notion of *esse*, allowed him a middle position between

Ibn-Sina and the Muslim religious thinkers (or the Franciscan voluntarists of the century following), who opposed the free and spontaneous divine will to a more intellectualist picture of creation.

The key to the medieval Christian voluntarists can be found in Scotus, whose epistemological predilections Gilson traces to Avicenna.[9] For he forebore any attempt to characterize the actual existence of things, treating that fact (like Aristotle) more like a presupposition then as something properly to be understood. What can be understood are essences, and the relations obtaining among them. That God *chooses* to make one arrangement of such essences to be the actual world turns on God's free choice —and that gives us contingency. So the contingency of things, for Scotus, lies not in their mode of being, but in the fact that they could have been otherwise: something is contingent "whose opposite could have occurred at the same time that this actually did."[10] A subtle difference from Aquinas, at first sight, for whom contingency resides in each thing receiving its proper to-be directly from the creator God. Yet on reflection, a vastly different relation is intimated between God and God's world. In the measure, of course, that that relationship may never find adequate expression, we must discover which models and analogies will be the least misleading ones. In that respect our inquiry reflects the spirit of the one whose position and writings linked Christians with Arabs: Moses Maimonides.

Epilogue

A CENTRAL PURPOSE OF this comparative study has been to show how the received doctrine of God in the West was already an intercultural, interfaith achievement. To be sure, one suspects that not even Aquinas, who executed the major act of synthesis, would have seen it that way. He seemed rather to have been imbued with an intrinsic respect for human understanding, inherited from the Greeks through the Arab *falasifa,* which counseled him to acknowledge truth wherever it may be found. It is, ironically enough, we who bring an intellectual presumption of otherness, to match what must have been Aquinas' religious sense of separation from Jew and Muslim. Medievals, for example, did not appear to share our preoccupations about the accuracy of translations, for they presumed that intelligent readers would grasp the sense of another intelligent writer—given the services of a creditable translator. And that presumption certainly proved true in the case of Aquinas, as the contemporary reader, served with critical texts of the Latin available to Aquinas as well as the Arabic original, can testify.

So the "conversation" elaborated in this story was never in fact a reciprocal one, yet communication took place, as Ibn-Sina influenced Maimonides, and both affected Aquinas. And our own experience of grappling with thinkers who have gone before us, in an attempt to understand *with them* a subject of concern to us both, should keep us from accepting historians' use of "influence" in too material a fashion. To acknowledge that another's thought has affected us is to recognize a debt of gratitude for the ways we have learned from our efforts to understand the other, rather than to give notice of material indebtedness. So despite the absence of face-to-face reciprocity, the enhancement is more akin to what happens in conversation than to passive reception. And if Aquinas was less aware of the *differences* which may have characterized his interlocutors than we, we are better equipped with critical editors and appraisals of their intellectual milieux than he was. So this study is intended to encourage us to capitalize on our rich resources, as he made do with what he had. For if we fancy ourselves in spirit and in fact ready to learn from other cultural and religious heritages, we can also find ourselves paralyzed by the multiple barriers which our cultivated sense of otherness has erected.

So I have deliberately focused on a single, if intractable, topic: the doctrine of God; and also selected philosophically-minded thinkers, who had at least serially grappled one with the other. That made the telling of a continuous story somewhat easier, though ever vulnerable as an account of intellectual history. After composing the narrative the way I have, and watching it emerge (as one does in writing), I realize *en passant* how many other ways it could be told. Islam is certainly not to be restricted to their *falasifa,* as we are constantly being reminded by Muslims themselves and astute students of Islam. They haven't even the corner on philosophical reflection in Islam.[1] Maimonides' specific concerns limited his systematic development, as we have noted, and one would need also to be led into less overtly philosophical areas of Jewish thought to have a fuller conception of their contribution to "theology."[2] So the story could be far richer, yet I have told it the way I have precisely to encourage others to amplify it as they can, utilizing other modes of thought and reflecting the turns the exchange takes in different times.

One result emerges clearly from this study, however, especially pertinent to philosophical inquiry today. The unity of God can hardly be comprehended as a purely philosophical assertion. For the phrase itself—"God is one" —is but shorthand for specific confessions of faith, and our manner of elucidating it should reflect the shape of those confessions: "Sh'ma, O Israel—Hear, O Israel, God your God is one..."/"I believe in one God, the Father almighty, creator of heaven and earth"/"There is no God but Allah . . ." The first is embedded in the story of Israel's becoming God's own people and so recalls a story of God; the second heads a list of chapter headings which articulate a Christian's faith by telegraphing the way Israel's story was continued and made over in Jesus; the last is ever recited in the midst of praises culling from the ninety-nine names of God the ones which recall Allah's mercy and presence to those whom the Qur'an has inspired.[3] To understand an apparently philosophical conclusion, then, one does best to try to identify the religious strands of which it is woven. Monotheism, once again, is not a confession but an abstraction. However convenient it may appear, one is ill-advised to assume it describes a common faith.

More generally still, apparently philosophical notions which recur for discussion in philosophy of religion, are never purely philosophical—whatever that could mean. Hence the need for inquiries such as this, to help the philosophically-minded appreciate the density and the multi-textured quality of these notions. I prefer to identify this sort of analysis with philosophical theology, to call attention to the fact that the analysis explicitly respects the elaboration of religious uses which has found its way into theology. Moreover, besides their historical (diachronic) dimension, these notions have a semantic (or synchronic) peculiarity as well, for they invariably incorporate analogical terms in their particular articulations. So an assessment of those formulae can never attend simply to questions of consistency. That is a *sine qua non,* of course, yet it can never dispense with a prior study of their literary texture, to try to pinpoint the sense in which they are intended. For ambiguities abound in these domains; and it is worth recalling just how *analogy* remained for Aquinas a species of ambiguity.

He never tried to domesticate analogical notions by finding a univocal thread of meaning linking the various identifiable uses. What seems to most modern writers to be the only way to offer analogy respectability would have rendered it superfluous for Aquinas. (Much like those analysts of metaphor who keep trying to spell them out non-metaphorically. Were their project realizable, metaphors would remain as decoration only.) What makes analogical expressions at once respectable and invaluable to Aquinas is our use of judgment. For it is judgment—of the same sort that selects an apt metaphor—which identifies the paradigm sense, and can discern how the other uses are "proportionally" related to that principal use. Moreover, the paradigm sense need never be fixed, so that discernment requires an active exercise of judgment. Nor can we expect to find an algorithm in recognizing "proportional" relatednesses, since *proportio* merely translates *analogia* here, and mathematical proportions are but a special subclass.

Here synchronic considerations merge with diachronic, semantics with history, as our attempts to identify paradigm senses at different times in diverse cultures demand that we enter into those times and cultures as best we can. And since that exploration is never finished, this sort of analysis can always profit from criticism—historical and philosophical, since it inextricably involves both disciplines. Yet the criticism will be more profitable, the more sensitive the inquiry has proven to the realities involved. The story may be shown to be awry, in other words, but those efforts will prove progressively illuminating in the measure that the approach itself of weaving a story of interaction is the one appropriate to the quest for understanding and for truth in these domains. It's because I trust the method that I look forward to the critics' response.

The crucial division in current philosophical discussion (in Anglo-American circles, at least) is not the traditional one between historians and philosophers—itself a deep temperamental difference; but between philosophers who find a diachronic study of permutations in meaning indispensable to establishing their point, and those who dispense with it handily. As Stephen Toulmin has reminded us, much of this can be traced quite simply (and historically) to diverse paradigms of graduate training, yet the philosophical consequences are immense.[4] It follows nearly exactly that those who can dispense with history must demand a clear, univocal sense for each expression, while those sensitive to historical shifts in meaning can appreciate the need for analogical uses. In any case, a comparative study such as this demands both historical awareness and analogical discernment. One of the goals of this inquiry has been to link the growing awareness we have of living in an intercultural situation with a philosophical approach attuned to realizing those resources.

Notes

PREFACE

1. Karl Rahner, S.J., "Towards a Fundamental Interpretation of Vatican II," *Theological Studies* 40 (1979) 716-27.

INTRODUCTION

1. The term "philosophical theology" embraces many of the issues once considered under "natural theology," but with less concern to distinguish between the sources—reason or revelation—and no specific apologetic intent.

2. Robert Sokolowski's *God of Faith and Reason* (Notre Dame, IN: University of Notre Dame Press, 1982) develops the role of distinctions in knowing, and clarifies this distinction specifically.

3. My *Aquinas: God and Action* (Notre Dame, IN: University of Notre Dame Press, 1979) offers a focal study of his grammatical way of pursuing these matters.

4. One may employ this term realizing that it is an abstraction, but it is well to avoid using it for the same reason.

5. Bernard J. F. Lonergan's *Insight* (London: Longmans, 1958) is the handbook for knowing as self-appropriation; Wilfred Cantwell Smith's *Towards a World Theology* (Philadelphia: Westminster, 1981) charts the course in an explicitly intercultural and interreligious context.

6. Sokolowski, 39.

1. PICTURING THE CONNECTION

1. *Critique of Pure Reason*, trans. N. K. Smith (London: Macmillan, 1961) Transcendental Dialectic, Bk. II, Ch. 3 [495-524].

2. Ibid., Section 7 [525-31].

3. From Alvin Plantinga's "Reason and Belief in God," in Alvin Plantinga and Nicholas Wolterstorff, eds., *Faith and Rationality* (Notre Dame, IN: University of Notre Dame Press, 1983) 16-93; to D. Z. Phillips' "Religious Beliefs and Language Games," in *Faith and Philosophical Enquiry* (London: Routledge and Kegan Paul, 1970) 77-110.

4. If we expect proofs to deliver a conclusion from the premises offered to assure such delivery. Yet if we consider their structure more carefully (moving from *effect* to *cause*, as he puts it), they could be construed as attempts to make inquirers aware of what their specific activity of inquiring presupposes. For a contemporary example of this approach, see Alastair MacKinnon's *Falsification and Belief* (The Hague: Mouton, 1970).

5. Nicholas Lash's introduction to John Henry Newman's *Grammar of Assent* (Notre Dame, IN: University of Notre Dame Press, 1979) offers an illuminating re-presentation of his thesis; see also my "Religious Belief and Rationality," in C. F. Delaney, ed., *Rationality and Religious Belief* (Notre Dame, IN: University of Notre Dame Press, 1979) for "retrospective justification."

6. Ernest Becker, like so many others, presumes this cultural feature in *Denial of Death* (New York: Free Press, 1973); but see John Coleman, S.J., "Situation for Modern Faith," *Theological Studies* 39 (1978) 601-32.

7. Loren Eiseley's, *Firmament of Time* (New York: Atheneum, 1980) develops this theme masterfully.

8. John Coulson's study: *Religion and Imagination* (Oxford: Clarendon Press, 1981).

9. Aquinas' classic texts are found in *In duodecim libros metaphysicorum Aristotelis expositio* (Torino: Marietti, 1950) L.VI, lectio 1 [1162-65]. For a sensitive commentary, see L.-B. Geiger, O.P., *Philosophie et Spiritualite* I (Paris: Cerf, 1963) 71-86.

10. *La divina commedia* III, 33 *ad fin.*

11. Stephen Toulmin offers a conciliating scheme in his *Uses of Argument* (Cambridge: Cambridge University Press, 1958).

12. A. Badawi, *Histoire de la philosophie en Islam II* (Paris: Vrin, 1972) 538-45, 648-56, 695.

13. The axiom itself offers a clear way of distinguishing emanation from creation, for when the latter is considered as an intentional act, nothing prohibits that act's producing many things.

14. Alfarabi offers an example of such comparative work in his *Philosophy of Plato and Aristotle*, ed. Muhsin Mahdi (Ithaca, NY: Cornell University Press, 1962).

15. J. L. Kraemer, "Alfarabi's *Opinions of the Virtuous City* and

Maimonides' *Foundations of the Law,"* in *Studio Orientalia memoriae D. H. Baneth dedicata* (Jerusalem: Magnes Press—Hebrew University, 1979) 107-53.

16. John Damascene, *De fide orthodoxa*: English translation by Frederic Chase, *St. John of Damascus, Writings* (Washington, D.C., Fathers of the Church, 1958).

17. Roger Arnaldez' introductory remarks in his *Grammaire et theologie chez Ibn Hazm de Cordone* (Paris: Vrin, 1956) offer helpful comparisons between Torah and *shar'ia* (9-16).

18. Such is Louis Gardet's judgment on Ibn Sina's mysticism: *La pensée réligieuse d'Avicene* (Paris: Vrin, 1951) 185-96.

19. In a comparative study entitled *Faith and Belief* (Princeton, NJ: Princeton University Press, 1979), Wilfrid Cantwell Smith raises these questions (esp. 51-52).

20. James W. McClendon and James M. Smith, *Understanding Religious Convictions* (Notre Dame, IN: University of Notre Dame Press, 1975).

21. *Sum. theol.* 1.45.5, *De potentia* 3.4.

22. S. A. Kamali, ed., *al-Ghazali's Tahafut al-Falasifah* (Lahore: Pahistan Philosophical Congress, 1958) 75-81 (Problem III).

23. Norbert Max Samuelson, trans. and ed., *Gersonides on God's Knowledge* (Toronto: Pontifical Institute of Medieval Studies, 1977) 232; also "Gersonides' Account of God's Knowledge of Particulars," *J. Hist. Phil.* 10 (1972) 399-416.

24. Compare Gardet's final critique of Ibn-Sina (note 18) with Gordon Kaufman's explicit intentions in *Theological Imagination* (Philadelphia: Westminster, 1981).

25. Roman numerals refer to chapters in P. Jaussen, Y. Karam, and J. Chala's edition of Alfarabi, *Idées des habitants de la Cité vertueuse* (Beirut: Librairie Orientale, 1980).

26. Robert Sokolowski, *God of Faith and Reason* (Notre Dame: University of Notre Dame Press, 1982); also his "Making Distinctions," *Review of Metaphysics* 32 (1979) 652-61.

27. So Ghazali, *Le tabernacle des lumières*, trad. Roger Deladriere (Paris: Seuil, 1981): "l'existence qui appartient a l'etre du fait d'un autre est un existence empruntee, et il ne subsiste pas par lui-meme" (52).

28. Such would be my critique of the "process theology" enterprise: "Does Process Theology Rest on a Mistake?" *Theol. Studies* 43 (1982) 125-35.

29. Avicenne: *La Metaphysique du Shifa*, trad. G. C. Anawati (Paris: Vrin, 1978) 108.

2. A CENTRAL DISTINCTION: ESSENCE/EXISTENCE

1. Louis Gardet, *La pensée réligieuse* 112-41.

2. *Shifa* 1.6; Anawati trans. 114-5.

3. *Shifa* 1.5; Anawati trans. 108.

4. P. F. Strawson, *Introduction to Logical Theory* (New York: John Wiley, 1960) 175-9.

5. Maimonides identifies Aristotle's teaching as "a branch deriving from his root doctrine concerning the eternity of the world," wherein unchanging species are preserved and individuals generally neglected (3.17, Pines 465).

6. This is the argument for Aquinas' interpretation being more faithful to the spirit of Aristotle, while acknowledging Averroes to be more literally faithful.

7. One thinks especially of Gabriel Marcel's philosophical and literary works, or of the novels of Tolstoy.

8. On this contested issue, see the discussion by D. F. Pears and James Thompson, in P. F. Strawson, ed., *Philosophical Logic* (Oxford: Oxford University Press, 1967) 97-106; the response to G. E. Moore's "Is Existence a Predicate?" in *Aristotelian Society* Suppl. Vol 15 (1936), and the symposium with W. Kneale, reprinted in *Philosophical Papers* (London: George Allen and Unwin, 1959) 114-25.

9. Cf. John S. Dunne, *Time and Myth* (Notre Dame, IN: University of Notre Dame Press, 1976) Ch. 1.

10. Cf. my "Kierkegaard: Language of Spirit," in *Exercises in Religious Understanding* (Notre Dame, IN: University of Notre Dame Press, 1974).

11. Cf. my "Jung: A Language for Soul" in *Exercises*.

12. Al-Ghazali, *Le tabernacle des lumières*, trad. Roger Deladriere (Paris: Seuil, 1981) 52-3.

13. *Shifa*, 1.8, Anawati trans. 123.

14. Ibid.

15. This captures the primacy which Aristotle attributes to the declarative sentence *asserting* what is the case; cf. my "Substance—a Performatory Account," in M. L. O'Hara, ed., *Substances and Things* (Washington, D.C., University Press of America, 1982) 224-29.

16. Anawati trans. (Introduction), 78.

17. *Shifa* 1.5, Anawati trans. 108 (Latin text renders *haqiqa: certitudo*).

18. Ibid.

19. *Shifa* 8.4 (Georges Anawati has translated the rest of the

Metaphysics, which will appear from Vrin in Paris. These translations are beholden to his, and the page and line references following will be to his Arabic edition: 344, 10–12). For Arabic use of *anniyya,* see R. M. Frank, "Origin of the Arabic Philosophical Term 'anniyya'": Musse Lavigerie: *Cahiers de Byrsa VI* (1956) 181–201 (Paris: Imprimerie Nationale, 1956).

20. *Shifa* 8.4. (346,12).

21. *Averroes' Tahafut al-Tahafut,* trans. Simon van den Bergh (Oxford: Oxford University Press, 1954) 178–80, 221–24, 238–41. See also Alexander Altmann, "Essence and Existence in Maimonides," in *Studies in Religious Philosophy and Mysticism* (London: Routledge and Kegan Paul, 1969) 108–27; and Fazlur Rahman, "Essence and Existence in Avicenna," in R. Hunt, R. Klibansky, L. Lobowsky, eds., *Medieval and Renaissance Studies* 4 (London, 1958) 1–16.

22. Anawati trans. 78: "By contrast, St. Thomas begins with the existing being and makes *esse* what is most intimate and profound in that being" (*Sum. theol.* 1.8.1.4).

23. Though Ibn-Sina gestures in that direction at 8.3 (342: 10–15): "What it means to say that a thing is created is that it receives its existence from another, ... thus everything is created with respect to the First Cause." Maimonides is preoccupied with distinguishing his position from Aristotle's regarding the eternity of the world (1.13–20) and from the Arabs regarding the necessity of emanation (1.21–24), introducing the fact of creation as Torah-revelation (1.25–27).

24. M.-D. Roland-Gosselin, *Le "de ente et essentia" de S. Thomas d'Aquin* (Kain, Belgique: La Saulchoir, 1926); Armand Maurer, *On Being and Essence,* 2nd revised ed. (Toronto: Pontifical Institute of Medieval Studies, 1968); Joseph Bobik, *Aquinas on Being and Essence* (Notre Dame, IN: University of Notre Dame Press, 1965).

25. *Shifa* 1.5; on essences considered "in themselves," see Fadlou Shehadi, *Metaphysics in Islamic Philosophy* (Delmar, NY: Caravan, 1982) 77–83.

26. A. M. Goichon, "The Philosopher of Being [Ibn-Sina]," *Avicenna Commemoration Volume* (Calcutta: Iran Society, 1956) 107–17.

27. L. de Raeymaeker, "L'être sélon Avicenne et sélon S. Thomas d'Aquin," in *Avicenna Commemoration Volume* (note 26) 119–32; so Ibn-Sina: "thus everything, except the one which is one by itself and exists by itself, derives its existence from another. It exists by that other yet in itself it is not" (8.3 [342:7–8]).

28. E. Gilson, "Avicenne et le point de départ de Duns Scot," *Archives d'Hist. Doct. Litt. du M-A.* 2 (1927) 89–149.

29. E. Gilson, "Le sources greco-arabes de l'Augustinianisme avicennisant," *Arch. d'Hist. Doct. Litt du M-A* 4 (1929-30) 5-107.

30. E. Gilson, "Pourquoi S. Thomas a critiqué S. Augustin," *Arch. d'Hist Doct. Litt du M-A* 1 (1926) 5-127.

31. Anawati trans. 78. He cites Gilson with approval: "No conciliation is possible between Avicennian extrinsicism and Thomist intrinsicism regarding existence; the passage from one to another cannot be one of evolution but requires a revolution" (*Le Thomisme* 5 ed. [Paris: Vrin, 1958] 58-59).

32. Despite their historical proximity—so the *prima facie* validity of David Kolb's surprise to find "an Aquinas who looks more like Wittgenstein than Avicenna" (*J. Religion* 61 [1981] 423-32) tends to lose its force on closer inspection.

33. Roland-Gosselin (note 24) 190, 192, 198.

34. See my "Maimonides, Aquinas and Gersonides on Providence and Evil," *Religious Studies* 20 (1984) 335-51.

35. De Raeymaeker (note 27) 128-29.

36. Among other references: *ST* 1.3.4, 44.1, 75.5, 104.1; *De malo* 16.3. Cf. de Raeymaeker, 129 n.1.

37. L.-B. Geiger, "Etre et Agir dans le philosophie de S. Thomas," in *Philosophie et Spiritualite* (Paris: Cerf, 1963) 159-81; also my *Aquinas: God and Action*, ch. 3.

38. Here I am beholden to B. J. F. Lonergan's detailed analysis of Aquinas' epistemology, in *Verbum: Word and Idea in Aquinas* (Notre Dame, IN: University of Notre Dame Press, 1967).

39. "Hoc est ergo quod addit verum supra ens, scilicet conformitatem, sive adaequationem rei et intellectus" (*De veritate* 1.1).

40. Joseph de Finance, *Etre et Agir* 2nd ed. (Rome: Gregorianium, 1960); cf. review by Geiger (note 37).

41. *Shifa* 8.3 (342:10-15).

42. *Shifa* 4.2 (182:10,14,17).

43. *S.T.* 1.46.1.1.; *De pot.* 3.1.2; cf. A. Faust, *Bulletin Thomiste* (1927) 146-7.

3. THE NATURE OF DIVINITY

1. ". . . the good . . . is the cause of . . . and even more splendid than knowledge and truth" (508e); "the source not only of the intelligibility of the objects of knowledge, but also of their being and reality, yet it is not itself that reality, but is beyond it" (509b)— Desmond Lee translation.

2. Georges Anawati, *La Metaphysique du Shifa*, 78; B. J. F.

Lonergan, *Insight* (London: Longmans, 1958)—cf. my "Method and Sensibility" *JAAR* 40 (1972) 349-67.

3. David Kolb, "Langauge and Metalanguage in Aquinas," *J. Religion* 61 (1981) 428-32.

4. See ch. 2, notes 28, 29, 30.

5. I prefer Timothy McDermott's translation of *simplicitas* as 'simpleness' because that unusual term suggests a "formal feature" (*Summa theologiae*, vol. 2: *Existence and Nature of God* [London: Eyre and Spotiswoode, 1964]). The distinction of such features from other attributes is developed in my *Aquinas: God and Action*, and also treated by Mark Jordan, "Names of God and the Being of Names," in Alfred J. Freddoso, ed., *Existence and Nature of God* (Notre Dame, IN: University of Notre Dame Press, 1983) 161-90.

6. "Hear, O Israel, God our God is one"; "There is no god but Allah"; and "I believe in one God. . . ."

7. *Shifa* 8.4; cf. Richard Frank (ch. 2, note 19).

8. *Idées de habitants* . . . (ch. 1, note 25) I, II, V, VII.

9. It is, moreover, an explicit philosophical "dig" at the incapacity of Islamic religious thought (*kalam*) to *show* the primacy of divinity—Louis Gardet, *La pensee religieuse*, 45-68.

10. Alfarabi (note 8) IV, V.

11. The climate of medieval thought allows us to speak of them as *interlocutors* with Aquinas. I have displayed this in a contrived dialogue: "Aquinas and Maimonides: A Conversation about Proper Speech," *Emmanuel* 16 (1983) 70-85.

12. Aquinas' structure of questions 3-11 is illustrative: "The ways in which God does not exist will become apparent if we rule out from him everything inappropriate, such as compositeness, change, and the like. Let us inquire then: first, about God's simpleness, thus ruling out compositeness. And then, because in the material world simpleness implies imperfection and incompleteness, let us ask secondly, about God's perfection; thirdly, about his limitlessness; fourthly, about his unchangeableness; fifthly, about his oneness."

13. And from diverse starting points: so Schubert Ogden in *Reality of God* (New York: Harper and Row, 1966) 59-65; and Alvin Plantinga, *Does God Have a Nature?* (Milwaukee, WI, Marquette University Press, 1980). I shall be more in dialogue with Plantinga in this chapter and the next, having met Ogden in *Aquinas: God and Action*, ch. 5; and more recently: "Does Process Theology Rest on a Mistake," *Theological Studies* 43 (1982) 125-35. See reply by Philip Devenish: "Post-Liberal Process Theology—A Rejoinder," ibid., 504-13.

14. Plantinga, 27.

15. Anthony Kenny, *The God of the Philosophers* (Oxford: Clarendon Press, 1979) 93.

16. E. Gilson, "Les sources . . ." (ch. 2, note 29).

17. A useful theological analogy might be found in the course of theological reflection on Luther's affirmation of *sola fide*: the more one speaks of faith, the more it is turned into something like a *work*!

18. So we must construe the potentially misleading assertions of *ST* 1.7.1.: "maxime formale omnium est ipsum esse," and 1.8.1: "cum [esse] sit formale respectu omnium quae in re sunt." McDermott nicely translates them: "the notion of form is most fully realized in existence itself" (1.7.1), and "for everything . . . is potential when compared to existence" (1.8.1).

19. *Revue Thomiste* 59 (1951) 335, 386.

20. Plantinga, 34.

21. For the notion of a "formal feature," see Edy Zemach, "Wittgenstein's Philosophy of the Mystical," *Review of Metaphysics* 18 (1964) 38–57.

22. Plantinga, 34.

23. This is the central argument of my *Aquinas: God and Action*.

24. Maimonides, *Guide for the Perplexed* 1.53–54; for Ibn-Sina, cf. Gardet, *La pensée réligieuse*, 41–42.

25. Ogden defends the analogy in *Reality of God* (note 13) 177–79.

26. That is, asserting that God is simple does not predicate a property of divinity, but calls our attention to a "formal feature" which qualifies all predication *in divinis*.

27. See precisions of note 18.

28. See my "God's Eternity," *Faith and Reason* 1 (1984).

4. NAMES OF GOD: ATTRIBUTES OF DIVINE NATURE

1. Cf. Abdurrahmann Badawi, *Histoire de la Philosophie en Islam* I (Paris: Vrin, 1972) 172–89.

2. Cf. Roger White, "Notes on analogical predication and speaking about God," in Brian Hebblethwaite and Stewart Sutherland, eds., *Philosophical Frontiers of Christian Theology* (Cambridge: Cambridge University Press, 1982) 197–226.

3. This is the central burden of Alvin Plantinga's *Does God Have a Nature?* (Milwaukee, WI: Marquette University Press, 1980). I shall be in conversation with Plantinga throughout this chapter.

4. See my "Aquinas and Maimonides: A Conversation about Proper Speech," *Immanuel* #16 (1983) 70–85.

5. See my *Aquinas,* ch. 12.

6. Ibid., ch. 4.

7. Ibid., ch. 2.

8. By "essential attributes" (Maimonides) we mean those which we cannot conceive "the beginning and end of all things" to lack, taken in itself—prescinding from relation to a gratuitous creation.

9. Armand Maurer, ed., *St. Thomas Aquinas "On Being and Essence"* (Toronto: Pontifical Institute of Medieval Studies, 1968), Introduction.

10. The citation is from *Summa contra gentiles* (= *CG*) 1.38; also *ST* 1.6.3.

11. Aquinas will employ the neo-Platonic scheme which divides being into *essential* and *participated,* without however endorsing any emanation scheme—cf. *ST* 1.4.3.3.

12. *CG* 1.73, *ST* 1.19.1.3, 1.20.3.2 Bernard Lonergan's treatment of the relations between knowing and willing in divinity, and the necessity for a *terminus ad extra contingens,* can be found in *Grace and Freedom* (New York: Herder and Herder, 1971).

13. Plantinga, *Nature?,* 34-35. This discussion of properties is part of a dialectical attempt to understand Aquinas' argument.

14. Alfarabi, *Les idees . . .* (ch. 1, note 25) I, II; Louis Gardet, *La pensée réligieuse,* 41-44.

15. Schlomo Pines, ed. and trans., *Guide of the Perplexed* (Chicago: University of Chicago Press, 1963) xlix.

16. *Guide* 1.61-62; Pines ed., xlix-1. On God's unknowability in the western medieval tradition, see Joseph Owens, "Aquinas—'Darkness of Ignorance' in the Most Refined Notion of God," in Robert Shahan and Francis Kovach, eds., *Bonaventure and Aquinas: Enduring Philosophers* (Norman, OK: University of Oklahoma Press, 1978) 69-86; also Mark Jordan, "Names of God and the Being of Names," in Alfred Freddoso, ed., *Existence and Nature of God* (Notre Dame, IN: University of Notre Dame Press, 1983) 161-90.

17. See the critique by Levi ben Gershon, in *Gersonides on God's Knowledge,* ed. Norbert Max Samuelson (Toronto: Pontifical Institute of Medieval Studies, 1977) 182-224.

18. *ST* 1.13.4, together with note by Herbert McCabe: "Imperfectly Signify," in *Summa theologiae* III (New York: McGraw-Hill, 1967); also my "Aquinas on Naming God," *Theological Studies* 24 (1963) 183-212.

19. Plantinga, *Nature?,* 4; see also 3-9, 34-37, where the discussion is nicely set up without taking sides.

20. Ibid.: "Now if we take the term 'property' in the very broad sense presently customary, this is of course paradoxical and plainly

false" (40). Yet why should we do so? It makes perfectly good sense to distinguish, as the medievals and as contemporary logic does, between properties and relations—as Plantinga's dialectical discussion displays (40–44).

21. Ibid., 34.
22. Ibid., 37. See Plantinga's discussion, 37–39.
23. Ibid., 4.
24. See my "God's Eternity," in *Faith and Philosophy* 1 (1984).
25. James Ross, "Creation II," in Freddoso (note 16).

5. GOD'S KNOWLEDGE OF PARTICULARS

1. 1.55. For the continuing discussion, see my "Maimonides, Aquinas, and Gersonides on Providence and Evil," *Religious Studies* 20 (1984) 335–51.

2. See Louis Gardet's assessment of the limits of mystical union in Ibn-Sina: *La pensée réligieuse,* 157–8, 185–96.

3. Gerard Verbeke, Introduction a *Avicenna Latinus: Liber de philosophia prima* V–X, ed. Simone van Riet (Leiden: Brill, 1980) 58*–59*.

4. See my "Creation, Will and Knowledge in Aquinas and Scotus," *Pragmatik* I, ed. H. Stachowiak (Hamburg: Felix Meiner, 1985).

5. Louis Gardet, "L'attitude philosophique d'Ibn-Sina," in *Livre Millenaire d'Avicenne* (Teheran, 1956) 93–103: "Il fut par la même confirmé dans une récherche de gnose intellectualiste et moniste, où Dieu Etre Necessaire, Lumière de lumière et Source des Lumières, se manifesterait en émanant nécessairement et voluntairement de toute éternité un monde contingent par essence" (98).

6. See Pines' discussion of the *prima facie* inconsistency here: I, xcvii–xcviii; Munk (*Guide des Egarés* [Paris: Maisonneuve, 1960]) attributes the source to Ibn-Sina (1.301–2, n. 4)—cf. *al-Shifa* 8.6, 358:10; although the original identification is Alfarabi's.

7. For a fascinating and instructive study of the background of Arab interpretation of Aristotle, see Edward Booth, O.P., *Aristotelian Aporetic Ontology in Islamic and Christian Thinkers* (Cambridge: Cambridge University Press, 1983).

8. Verbeke (note 3) 35*, 66*. Al-Ghazali makes a similar observation: "everything other than God is . . . unreal (*batl*) in its essence and real (*haqq*) by other than itself. Thus the absolutely real is the self-existing one, and from that one everything receives its reality (*haqiqa*)—*al Masad al-Asna,* ed. Fadlou Shehadi (Beirut: Librairie Orientale, 1980), 137.

9. Al-Kindi, "On the True, First and Perfect Agent, and the Imperfect Agent, which is only called Agent Metaphorically," in *Rasa'il al-Kindi al-falsafiyyah*, ed. Abu Ridah, 2 vols. (Cairo, 1950–53) I, 182–4; translation in A. Altmann and S. M. Stern, *Isaac Israeli* (Oxford: Oxford University Press, 1958) 68–69. Cf. A. Cortaberria O.P., "Un traite philosophique d'al-Kindi, *Mélanges d'Institut Dominicain des Etudes Orientales* (MIDEO) 12 (1974) 5–12.

10. Louis Gardet, *Dieu et la destinée de l'homme* (Paris: Vrin, 1967) 35–77, and Harry A. Wolfson, *Philosophy of the Kalam* Harvard: Harvard University Press, 1976) 655–719.

11. "[Aristotle] does not mean to say that the existence of the Universe is the necessary product of the Creator, i.e., the Prime Cause, in the same manner as the shadow is caused by a body, or heat by fire, or light by the sun, [namely, physical necessity]. Only those who do not understand his words attribute such ideas to him. He uses the term necessary in the same sense as we use the term when we say that the existence of the *intellectus* necessarily implies that of the *intellectum*, for the former is the efficient cause of the latter in so far as *intellectum* [i.e., logical necessity]" (2.20). Cf. Munk (note 6) II, 167 n. 1.

12. Cf. Munk (note 6) III, 116 n. 1.

13. Charles Kahn spells out the difference as succinctly as I have seen it:

My general view of the historical development is that existence in the modern sense becomes a central concept in philosophy only in the period when Greek ontology is radically revised in the light of a metaphysics of creation: that is to say, under the influence of Biblical religion. As far as I can see, this development did not take place with Augustine or with the Greek Church Fathers, who remained under the sway of classical ontology. The new metaphysics seems to have taken shape in Islamic philosophy, in the form of a radical distinction between necessary and contingent existence: between the existence of God, on the one hand, and that of the created world, on the other. The old Platonic contrast between Being and Becoming, between the eternal and the perishable (or, in Aristotelian terms, between the necessary and the contingent), now gets reformulated in such a way that for the contingent being of the created world (which was originally present only as a "possibility" in the divine mind) the property of "real existence" emerges as a new attribute or "accident," a kind of added benefit bestowed by God upon possible beings in the act of creation. What is new here is the notion of radical contingency, not simply the old Aristotelian idea that many things might be other than they in fact are—that many events might turn out otherwise—but that the whole world of nature might not have been created at all: that it might not have existed. ("Why Existence Does not Emerge as a Distinct Concept in Greek Philosophy," in Parviz Morewedge, ed., *Philosophies of Existence* [New York: Fordham University Press, 1982] 7-8).

14. The phrase is Gersonides':—see my article (note 1) and Norbert Max Samuelson, "Gersonides' Account of God's Knowledge of Particulars," *J. Hist. Phil.* 10 (1972) 399-416. Isaac Israeli (d. 955) had proposed a not unsimilar view: that *"creatio ex nihilo* ends with intellect, and emanation does the rest" (171)—Altmann and Stern (note 9).

15. See my "Essence and Existence: Avicenna and Greek Philosophy," *MIDEO* (1985), an analysis corroborated by Fadlou Shehadi in *Metaphysics in Islamic Philosophy* (Delmar, NY: Caravan, 1982) 93-100, 109-11.

16. On Ibn-Sina's "mysticism," see Louis Gardet, *La pensée réligieuse*, 153-96.

17. See Gersonides' *The Wars of the Lord—Treatise Three: On God's Knowledge* (Toronto: Pontifical Institute of Medieval Studies, 1977) 182-224.

18. Hence Sokolowski can call "the distinction" a "Christian distinction," even though it logically belongs to Judaism and to Islam as well, since it was the Christological controversies which forced its clearest articulation. See his *God of Faith and Reason*, pp. 31-40. The Chalcedonian formula can be found in H. Denzinger, ed., *Enchiridion symbolorum* (Rome: Herder, 1957) #148. It is ironic, though understandable, that liberal Christianity's aversion to the metaphysics of incarnation should have contributed to the search for a new metaphysics in Christian theology; see my "Is Process Theology based on a Mistake?" *Theological Studies* 43 (1982) 125-35.

19. *De diversis questionibus* LXXXIII, 46, 1-2 (Patrologia Latina 40, col 29-30). E. Gilson discusses the issue in his *Introduction a l'étude de Saint Augustin* (Paris: Vrin, 1931) 109-10, 257-58.

6. ETERNAL CREATOR OF CONTINGENT THINGS

1. S. Munk (Ch. 5, n. 6) has a wonderful citation from Saint Jerome (*S. Hieronymi Opera*, ed. Marteanay, t. III, col. 1600) in support of Maimonides restricting providence to human individuals (III, 131 N.1). Aquinas' treatment in *De ver.* 5.3 says that providence extends to individuals only in function of the species. Since the

context invites us to understand this of non-human beings, this treatment closely parallels Maimonides.

2. This is the thesis of Charles Kahn, "Why Existence does not Emerge as a Distinct concept in Greek Philosophy," in Parviz Morewedge, ed., *Philosophies of Existence* (New York: Fordham University Press, 1982) 7-17.

3. *How to do Things with Words* (Cambridge, MA: Harvard University Press, 1962) Lecture XII.

4. See my article (note 1) and also "God's Eternity," *Faith and Reason 1* (1984) 389-405.

5. As Al Plantinga does in closing his presidential address to the Western Division of the American Philosophical Association: "How to be an Anti-Realist," *APA Proceedings* 56 (1982) 47-70.

6. On *haecceitas,* see my "Creation, Will and Knowledge in Aquinas and Scotus," in *Pragmatik* I, ed. H. Stachowiak, (Hamburg: Felix Meiner, 1985). On *scientia media,* see Robert M. Adams, "Middle Knowledge and the Problem of Evil," *American Philosophical Quarterly* 14 (1977) 109-17.

7. See W. Norris Clarke, S.J., *The Philosophical Approach to God* (Winston-Salem, NC: Wake Forest University Press, 1979).

8. Cf. Charles Kahn (note 21).

9. See Ch. 2, notes 28-30.

10. *Opus Oxoniense* (Ordinatio), ed. Balic (Vatican City, 1954) I, d.2, q.1, a.2 ad 2; Allan Wolter, ed., *Duns Scotus: Philosophical Writings* (Edinburgh: Nelson, 1962) 55.

EPILOGUE

1. Roger Arnaldez, "Trouvailles Philosophiques Dans Le Commentaire Coranique De Fakhr Al-Din al-Razi," *Etudes Philosophiques et Litteraires* 3 (1968 [= Colloque Maghrebin de Philosophie, Rabat, 1968] 11-24.

2. A term Jews tend to shy away from, because of its historical associations with Christianity. Wilfrid Cantwell Smith, however, in his *Towards a World Theology* (Philadelphia: Westminster, 1981) offers a way of understanding 'theology' which respects the particular contributions of respective religious traditions without having to modify the term itself with the adjective naming that tradition. He takes us some way in learning how to think of ourselves as doing in our time what Aquinas certainly considered himself to be doing in his: "not a 'Christian theology'. . . but a Christian view of theology, a Christian interpretation of faith" (125).

3. Since a confession of faith usually lacks the precision of honed doctrinal formulations, yet must be concise to play the role it does, it is fruitful to consider them as chapter titles recalling the stories which embody the view of God and the divine perspective on human affairs which those titles then evoke.

4. Stephen Toulmin, *Human Understanding* I (Princeton, NJ: Princeton University Press, 1972) 156-65. See also Alasdair MacIntyre's "Response to Critics" appended to the revised edition of *After Virtue* (Notre Dame: University of Notre Dame Press, 1984).

Index

Abstract objects, 66–69
Accident, 26–27
Act, 31, 34, 49, 64, 96, 106
Actus essendi, 28, 30, 59–60, 94
Adams, R. M., 126
Agent, 77, 79
Alfarabi, *see* al-Farabi
Altmann, A., 118
Analogy, 37, 47, 75, 98, 112
Anawati, G., 26, 29, 36, 43
Aristotle, 8–9, 20, 36, 43, 46, 66, 73, 75, 80, 82
Arnaldez, R., 116, 126
Asharite, 83, 84
Attributes, 52, 54, 56–65, 86
Augustine, 89
Austin, J. L., 96

Badawi, A., 115, 121
Barth, K., 17
Becker, E., 115
Being, necessary/possible, 71, 80
Bobik, J., 118
Booth, E., 123

Capacity, 55–56
Clarke, W. N., 126
Coleman, J., 115
Contingency, 107–8
Cortaberria, A., 124
Coulson, J., 115
Creation, 15, 33–34, 75–80, 88

Dante, 8, 14
Distinction, of God from world, 2, 7, 17–18, 24, 46–47, 64–65, 68, 70, 75–76, 78, 79, 89; essence/existence, 26, 34, 35, 36, 39, 94, 106
Dunne, J., 117
Duns Scotus, 28, 38, 108

Eiseley, L., 115
Emanation, 9, 16, 28, 33, 45, 49, 73, 75
Esse, 29–32, 33, 42–45, 48, 59–61, 91, 94–96, 103–4, 106–7
Essence, 28, 29, 35, 37, 38, 43, 45, 66; -/existence: *see* Distinction; of God, 22, 44, 49, 58
Eternity, 50, 101, 105–6
Existence, 21–22, 26–27, 41, 46, 67, 91; -/essence: *see* Distinction; of God, 5; necessary, 40, 72
Existent, necessary, 24

al-Farabi, 9–10, 11–13, 28, 35, 40, 60, 62, 64, 74, 76–78, 85, 91–92
Formal feature, 38, 46–62, 98, 100, 103, 105
Frank, R., 118
Freedom, 104
Future contingencies, 99–105

ARABIC TERMS